$10

GAR 3-3

Modern Ocean Cruising

Modern Ocean Cruising

Boats, Gear and Crews Surveyed

JIMMY CORNELL

ADLARD COLES LIMITED
GRANADA PUBLISHING
London Toronto Sydney New York

Published by Granada Publishing in
Adlard Coles Limited 1983

Granada Publishing Limited
Frogmore, St Albans, Herts AL2 2NF
and
36 Golden Square, London W1R 4AH
515 Madison Avenue, New York, NY 10022, USA
117 York Street, Sydney, NSW 2000, Australia
100 Skyway Avenue, Rexdale, Ontario M9W 3A6, Canada
61 Beach Road, Auckland, New Zealand

British Library Cataloguing in Publication Data

Cornell, Jimmy
    Modern ocean cruising.
1. Yachts and yachting
I. Title
797.1'24   GV813

ISBN 0 229 11687 6

Printed in Great Britain by
Mackays of Chatham Ltd

Granada ®
Granada Publishing ®

FOR GWENDA

Many ocean cruises owe their success
to the seawife as much as to the skipper.
This book is dedicated to my seawife,
without whom it would never have
been written.

Contents

List of Maps and Diagrams

Introduction

Ocean voyaging is no longer the privilege of the few or the extraordinary, as more and more people undertake extended cruises across the oceans of the world. Over the years the design of boats has changed considerably, new materials have become available, instruments have reached a high level of sophistication and even old established concepts of seamanship have come under scrutiny. However the sea and the challenge it presents to the ocean voyager has remained the same. This challenge is one reason why many people put to sea. Cruising to faraway places has other attractions too, besides a desire to battle with the elements; it is also a means of escaping from the frustrations and stresses of modern society. Fortunately there are still many places which can only be reached by sea and the satisfaction of sailing one's own boat to such a place makes every sacrifice worthwhile. Many ocean voyagers are pursuing a dream and few of those who manage to realise it are disillusioned. To make this dream come true requires a lot of preparation and determination, and the ultimate success of a long distance cruise often depends on these initial preparations.

In pursuit of the dream of freedom myself, I started serious preparation for a world cruise in the early 1970's. I chose a Trintella III A, designed by Van der Stadt, for its sturdiness and suitable accommodation for a family with two young children. A limited budget forced me to buy just the bare hull, but fortunately I insisted on the best I could afford and the strong fibreglass hull built by the Tyler Boat Company has proved its worth on many occasions. After two years of fitting out the 36-footer, we set off from England in the spring of 1975. Six years later *Aventura* successfully completed her circumnavigation, having taken myself, my wife Gwenda and children Doina and Ivan on a voyage of 58,000 miles during which we visited over 50 countries in five continents.

When I left London I gave up my job with the BBC External Service, although I continued my radio work on a freelance basis throughout the voyage. This work encouraged me to visit many out of the way places; what started off as a three year trip took twice as long to complete. Like countless sailors before us, the South Seas cast their spell and if it hadn't been for the problem of our growing children's education, *Aventura* would still be sailing among the islands of the South Pacific.

When I started preparing for my voyage, I had little cruising experience, so I read avidly every available book on this subject. There were several books on the market, but most of them had one major drawback, they reflected the point of view of only one person, the author. They tended to be subjective, sometimes dogmatic, and seldom gave alternative points of view a good hearing.

After several years of sailing in the company of people who have made cruising their way of life, I came to realise that there was a fund of knowledge from these experienced sailors waiting to be tapped. Not wanting to fall into the same trap of preaching from the cockpit, I decided to try and let these sailors tell their own stories.

My training as a radio reporter showed me the obvious way, which was to let the people talk and for me to listen. The result of some three years of listening to countless skippers, mates and crews is included in these pages. In an attempt to be objective I carried out several surveys on specific subjects among the long distance cruising people that I encountered during my own voyage around the world. Each survey was based on a detailed questionnaire and the interviews were conducted in a systematic fashion. Wherever possible I tried to interview people on their own, preferably on their boats, as I found that people spoke more freely and honestly when others were not around. I attempted to process some of the data from the questionnaires in a simple statistical way by averaging figures and calculating percentages.

Although I tried to make the questionnaires as comprehensive and wide ranging as possible, some aspects had to be left out and when some of those interviewed felt strongly about certain overlooked points, I made a note of these. At the end of each interview, I also asked for general comments relating to the subjects under discussion and suggestions for others intending long distance voyages. Some of the most valuable information came to light in this way.

These 'surveys', as I call them, carried out over a number of years, form the basis of this book. Generally I have endeavoured to present the data resulting from the surveys in an unbiased way, only interpreting it when necessary. Of course I hold strong opinions myself on most of these matters, so I have tried to make it clear when I stray across the thin line of objectivity by expressing my own views or making a certain point by drawing on my own experience.

There were four main surveys:

1. *The Suva Survey.* The first survey of 62 cruising boats was conducted

MAP A Track of *Aventura's* voyage

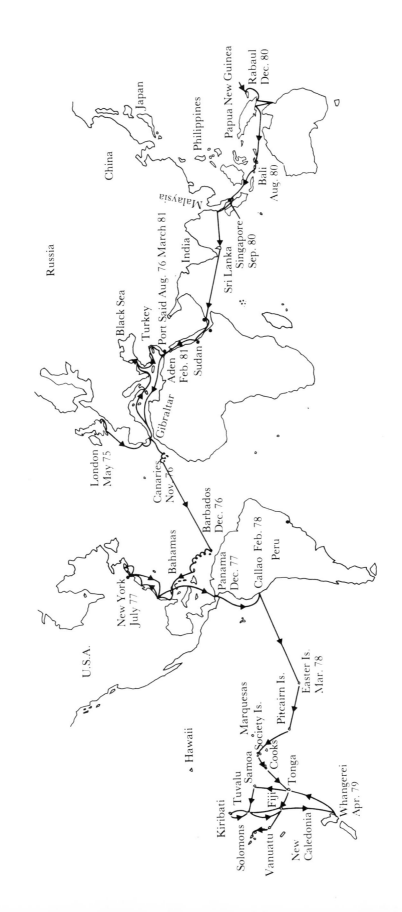

entirely in Suva, Fiji and dealt with various aspects of cruising boat design.

2. *The Cruising Survey*. The following year in a variety of places in the Pacific I conducted a more extensive survey among fifty long distance cruising boats. This dealt particularly with aspects of seamanship and the practical side of cruising.

3. *The Seawives Survey*. A separate survey was conducted parallel to the Cruising Survey among the cruising women.

4. *The Circumnavigation*. Twelve crews who had successfully completed their circumnavigation rounded off this series of surveys.

Tables showing the details of all these surveys are at the end of the book.

Although I gathered most of my material in the Pacific, I consider it applicable to any cruising area of the world. The people sailing in the Pacific are nearly all long distance voyagers, both they and their boats are well tried, their crews being committed to living aboard for long periods of time. They are all used to long offshore passages as distances in the Pacific are so vast that a 1000 mile passage between islands is commonplace. At the same time those cruising in the South Pacific have few facilities at their disposal, such as rescue services, port and repair facilities, navigational aids, even detailed and accurate charts. Of necessity in the Pacific, the sailor has to be more self-reliant.

Many of the people I interviewed had also sailed extensively in other oceans and the information they gave me was based on knowledge gained worldwide. Apart from these surveys, I have also drawn extensively from general conversations I have had with many skippers and letters written by the people concerned. There are many interesting people sailing the oceans of the world and they all have a story to tell. This is their tale.

CHAPTER ONE

In Search of the Ideal Boat

There are certain ports on the crossroads of the oceans rarely missed by any long distance cruising boats and one of these is Suva, the capital of Fiji. In September and October this excellent port, conveniently placed halfway across the South Pacific, is particularly crowded as the safe cruising season draws to its close and the cyclone season approaches. Many boats are preparing for a passage to New Zealand or Australia out of the cyclone area, while others staying in Suva find themselves a protected corner close to a hurricane hole to sit out the season. A few may carry on cruising, a gamble which had fatal results for two boats in 1979.

The anchorage off the Royal Suva Yacht Club, Fiji, a meeting place for long distance cruising boats.

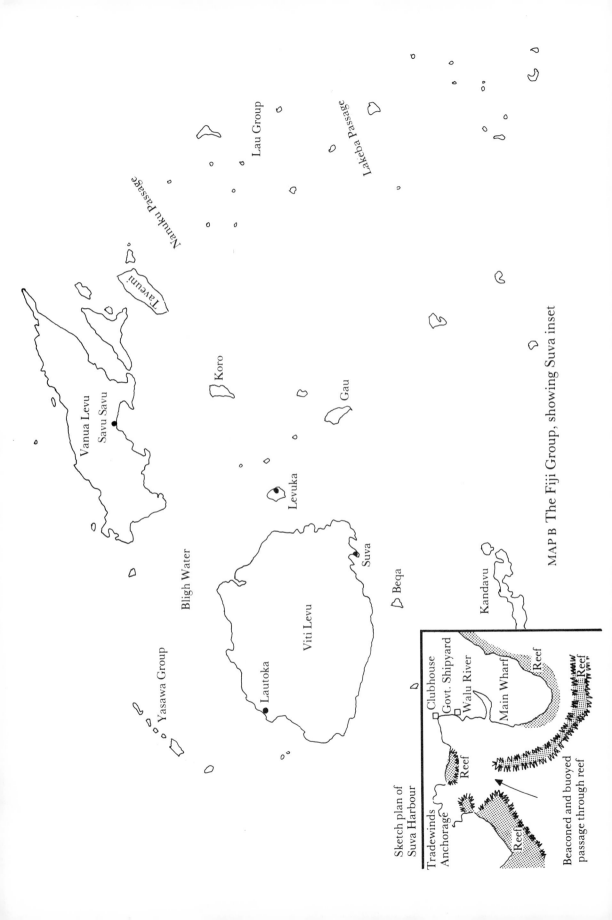

Nanuku Passage

Lau Group

Lakeba Passage

Taveuni

Vanua Levu

Savu Savu

Koro

Bligh Water

Gau

Yasawa Group

Levuka

Viti Levu

Suva

Lautoka

Beqa

Kandavu

MAP B The Fiji Group, showing Suva inset

Sketch plan of Suva Harbour

Tradewinds Anchorage

Clubhouse

Govt. Shipyard

Walu River

Main Wharf

Reef

Reef

Reef

Reef

Beaconed and buoyed passage through reef

Looking at the variety of boats anchored off the hospitable Royal Suva Yacht Club set me wondering where all the ideal blue water cruising boats were, those advertised in the glossy magazines and exhibited at boat shows. Maybe they were all cosily tucked away in expensive marinas in Europe and North America, certainly those sailing the oceans were a motley collection of different shapes, sizes and rigs, old and new, big and small.

In a search for the 'ideal' long distance cruising boat, I decided to try and find out in a statistical way what boats people were actually cruising in, and more importantly, what they thought about their boats. Hopefully, with a large enough sample some general conclusions could be drawn. Suva was an ideal place to begin and I tried to interview the skipper of every long distance cruising boat that came through during my own three month stay there.

Choosing the Sample

Only boats which had sailed a minimum of 2000 miles or who had been cruising for over three months were interviewed and sixty-two boats made up my first survey. In fact I soon discovered that most of the boats had been sailing for much further and longer, most of them over one year and up to fifteen years continuous cruising in the case of *Coryphena*. Three of the boats, *Warna Carina*, *Benn Gunn*, and *Sarrie*, were completing their circumnavigation, while Seaton Grass was taking his father's ketch *Merry Maiden* around the world a second time, having learned the ropes on a previous circumnavigation skippered by his father. The mileage covered by the boats on their present cruise worked out at an average of 15,000 miles per boat and the average length of the cruise so far was 2·6 years. It was soon apparent that many skippers were even more experienced, having sailed extensively before the present cruise. The sailing experience of all the skippers added up to a total of 856 years, quite a biblical age, being an average of 13·8 years per skipper. This considerable experience, together with the length of the cruises currently being undertaken gives immense authority to the answers obtained.

Size of Boat

The first thing I looked at was the size of the boats, which varied between two schooners over 70 ft long to a small sloop of only 24 ft. When I asked the skippers to give a rating to the design and sailing performance of their boats, I asked them to also take into account the size of the boat for the number of crew carried. Children were only counted as crew when they lived permanently on board and crews joining a boat for a limited period were excluded. The ratings were counted from one to ten, ten being the highest rating.

TABLE 1. *Results of optimum size questionnaire, Suva Survey.*

Length (ft)	Number of boats	Average number of crew	Average rating
under 35 ft	12	2	7·75
35–40 ft	22	2·5	9·27
40–45 ft	12	2·4	8·83
over 45 ft	16	3·5	9·25

The happiest skippers were those of boats in the 35–40 ft range (see Table 1) who rated their boats at an average of 9·27. The skippers of the twelve smaller boats, under 35 ft, gave their boats a lower rating of 7·75. Although the boats over 45 ft also received a high average rating, many of these had larger crews and in several cases where the crew consisted only of a couple, these skippers complained that their boats were too large to handle. For this reason, some of the larger boats took on temporary crew for longer passages.

The following year, during my second survey, consisting of fifty boats, the average cruising boat turned out to be in the same range, 38 ft long and with an average crew of 2·4, although I did not ask these skippers for a general rating of their boats.

Later, in a survey of twelve boats which had successfully completed their circumnavigation, mostly with a crew of two people, I found the boats to be of a slightly smaller size, on average 35 ft. Of these twelve, only two were over 40 ft, while three were under 30 ft. Asked to give an overall assessment of their boats, every single skipper specified that he was happy with his boat, having made the right choice for the voyage he undertook and the money he had available. That these twelve circumnavigating skippers were satisfied with their particular boat was to be expected, for these were the successes, not the failures, and their boats had all brought them safety back home. However out of these twelve, only four planned to keep their present boat, whilst all the other eight were planning or already building slightly larger boats for the future. Jean-Francois Delvaux of *Alkinoos*, who has

The skipper of *Lookfar* being interviewed by the author for the survey on cruising boats. Whenever possible the interviews took place on the boat in question.

sailed his 48 ft ketch virtually single-handed around the world, considers a boat of 38–40 ft long to be ideal for a world cruise. His view is shared by Herbert Gieseking who circumnavigated in his 31 ft *Lou IV* but is now replacing her with a 40 ft steel ketch, already well on the way to completion.

It has often been said that a short-handed crew should try and keep to a small boat, possibly under 35 ft overall. The Suva survey however showed that with only three exceptions every owner of a boat under 35 ft long complained about the small size and stated unreservedly that he would have preferred to have had a larger boat for this type of cruising. As to the difficulty of handling a larger boat, it was interesting to note that not a single boat in the 35–46 ft range with a crew of two was considered too difficult to handle, even in the worst conditions. Perhaps I should add that a lot of the crews were not all that young either, several being in their sixties. Alan Allmark, who has been cruising many years on his 35 ft *Telemark*, advised those choosing a long distance cruising boat, 'Don't go for a

Alan and Beryl Allmark have been cruising for many years on their 35 ft *Telemark*. They consider this to be an ideal size for a small crew.

bigger boat than you might need and most certainly do not buy a large boat just because you can afford it.'

Obviously the choice of the size of a boat depends greatly on the number of people who will be cruising in her. Bill and Frances Stocks were quite happy with their 30 ft cutter *Kleena Kleene II* until the birth of their daughter in Papua New Guinea, an event not foreseen when they had left British Columbia a few years previously. The boat then appeared to shrink rapidly as the pile of baby paraphernalia grew. Similarly *Warna Carina* left Australia with three small children aboard, but completed the circumnavigation with three large teenagers. By the time they had reached Suva, this family of five were finding their 36 ft boat overcrowded. Growing children *do* take up more space, and this is a factor to be considered in the choice of a family boat.

Long distance cruising boats usually spend more time at anchor than at sea, and this is when more space is important. Even in the tropics, where one may expect to spend most of the time in the open, an airy interior and spacious galley are essential. From the number of cruising folk who sleep in the cockpit on hot tropical nights, a large and comfortable cockpit would appear to be popular, also pleasant for entertaining visitors from other boats and from ashore. A cruising boat, after all, is a home as well as a sailing machine.

The often debated point of a centre versus an after cockpit seemed to be dictated often by the size of the boat, more of the smaller boats having an after cockpit then the larger ones. The people who had a centre cockpit and an after cabin all appeared pleased with this arrangement, often for the privacy gained when they had a crew. My own boat has a centre cockpit, which I always regarded as safer and more secure when my children were young, a point which has been mentioned to me by several parents. Otherwise the positioning of the cockpit did not appear to be a major consideration among those surveyed.

What was more important was that the helmsman had some sort of protection. In the Suva survey, six boats had a permanent doghouse or wheelhouse, while forty were provided with some kind of canvas dodger, which also gave protection to the main companionway and was usually left in position, even if it could be folded away. All skippers agreed that a protected steering position was an essential fixture on any cruising boat however much one relied on selfsteering or autopilot. Almost all of the few skippers who had unprotected cockpits wished that they had some protection and mentioned that it was high on their list of jobs to be done at the first opportunity.

The carrying capacity of a larger boat was another consideration mentioned by many of those interviewed, as stores, books and souvenirs always weigh more than designers allow for. Every smaller boat which had been away from base for longer than a year looked as though it was sinking under the added weight. Also, as some of these skippers pointed out, with a little more storage space available, stores can be bought where they are cheapest. In these days of continuous inflation, when most boats start off on a long cruise with a fixed amount of money, it is often a wise investment to buy certain goods where and when they are conveniently priced. There are still a handful of ports around the world where one can buy most provisions and duty free liquor at knockdown prices, if one has the cash and space available.

Hull Form

The demand for more spaciousness has resulted in modern cruising boats being generally beamier and having more freeboard than older designs. In the Suva survey the ratio of beam to length was less for older boats. The overall ratio of beam to length on deck for the 57 monohulls was 30·8 per cent, being higher for the smaller sized boats.

TABLE 2. *Results of hull shape analysis, Suva Survey.*

Size of boat	Number of boats	Average draft	Ratio of beam to length (LOD)
over 50 ft	7	8 ft	26·4%
40–50 ft	18	6 ft	29·6%
30–40 ft	25	5·4 ft	31·2%
under 30 ft	7	4·4 ft	33·2%

Similar conclusions could be drawn in the case of draft, where as to be expected the larger the boat the deeper the draft. Although the skippers were not asked to rate the draft of their boats, a deeper draft was often mentioned as a disadvantage in certain cruising areas. This was one of the reasons why the majority had chosen a long keel rather than a fin keel, as boats fitted with the latter type of keel tend to draw more.

Among the 57 monohulls, 39 had a long keel, which was rated an average of 8·96. The 8 boats with a medium keel were rated 9·12, while the 8 fin keelers received an average rating of 8·93. Two of the smaller boats had bilge keels, which they rated at 6·5. Among the boats classified as long keelers, three had centreboards, two of their owners expressing some reservations about this arrangement, because of troubles they had had with lowering and raising the board.

TABLE 3. *Results of keel analysis, Suva Survey.*

Size of boat	Keel Shape							
	Long		Medium		Fin		Bilge	
	No.	Ave. Rating	No.	Ave. Rating	No.	Ave. Rating	No.	Ave. Rating
over 40 ft	19	9·3	4	9·25	2	10	–	
30–40 ft	16	9·0	4	9·0	4	9·0	1	6
under 30 ft	4	7·0	–		2	7·5	1	7
totals	39	8·96	8	9·12	8	8·93	2	6·5

Another reason why so many people chose a long keel was its better suitability for cruising, they being prepared to sacrifice some speed in return for a sturdier underwater profile. Most owners of long keel boats consider a fin keel to be a weak point, although the skippers of the fin keelers in the Suva survey were all satisfied with this type of keel.

Beam, freeboard, hull shape and draft are all functions of the overall size of the boat and my general impression, after concluding the various surveys, was that most cruising people are less interested in the particular aspects of boat design than racing people are. They choose their boats for the overall aesthetic and functional design and are quite happy to leave the finer points of naval architecture to the designers. Perhaps cruising people should show more interest in boat design, for I feel that in recent years, too many racing features have crept into cruising boat design, which are not necessarily an improvement for cruising requirements. A case in point is the tendency to less and less protected rudders, some designers even dispensing with a skeg altogether.

General considerations similarly seem to dictate the choice of a mono or multihull. Out of the 62 boats in the Suva survey, five were multihulls and the average rating given to their overall design was 7·8, as compared to the average rating of 8·6 given to the 57 monohulls. Generally multihulls do not appear to be so popular among the long distance voyagers, as many skippers still express serious reservations about the general safety of multi-hulls for this type of voyaging. It is certainly my own opinion that the obvious advantages of multihulls, such as speed, spaciousness and moderate draft, do not make up for my doubts that even a well designed multihull may not stand up to the extreme conditions that one may encounter in long distance ocean voyaging.

The Rig

After the size and satisfaction with the general design of the boat, the question of rig was considered. In the Suva survey, exactly half of the boats were single-masted, generally the smaller ones. All the skippers were very firm in their assessment of the particular rig they carried and were precise in outlining its advantages or shortcomings. Overall, cutters received the highest ratings (see Table 4) and a number of sloop owners specified that they would have preferred a cutter to a sloop for extended cruising. Among the ketches, the twelve that were provided with a boomed staysail were rated higher by their owners (average rating 8·38), than the ketches without a staysail (7·86), most owners of the latter type stating that they

The eyecatching schooner *Sea Swan* at anchor in Suva, designed and built by the owner Miles Corener with traditional beauty in mind.

would have preferred a staysail arrangement. Two boats were able to hoist a staysail on a provisional inner forestay, which could be moved back to the mast when not needed. As for the schooners, it was interesting to note that the rig was rated as low as 2 by a shorthanded skipper while, at the other extreme, a schooner with a crew of eight was rated the maximum 10. One disgruntled skipper, Miles Corener, who had built his *Sea Swan* from scratch with timber chosen and hewn out himself from the forests of Connecticut, was honest to admit, 'I only chose a schooner rig for its looks.' The third schooner was also rated highly by the skipper who used a square sail extensively, especially when shorthanded.

TABLE 4. *Results of rig questionnaire, Suva Survey.*

Type of rig	Number	Percentage of total	Average LOD (ft)	Average rating
Sloop	19	31%	33	8·58
Cutter	12	19%	39	9·25
Ketch	27	44%	42	8·10
Yawl	1	1·6%	42	5
Schooner	3	5%	67	7·33

In the Cruising survey, cutters were equally popular, making up almost half of the one-masted boats. Again the two masted boats were generally the larger ones, there being twenty ketches, one schooner and one yawl.

The dozen successful circumnavigators, who on the whole sailed smaller than average boats, comprised eight sloops, one cutter and three ketches. Three of the sloop owners did specify that their next boat would definitely be a cutter. The two larger boats over 40 feet were both ketches, the third ketch being the 31 foot long Jensen design, *Lou IV*. This Danish-designed ketch was surprisingly spacious and well proportioned for its length, with its after cabin and two masts.

The cutter *Runestaff* tacking past *Lou IV*, *Hägar* and *Rhodora* in Suva harbour. For long distance cruising, a cutter is regarded by most skippers as the most suitable rig.

Many of the larger boats were two-masted as much for aesthetic as for practical reasons, especially those with an after cabin where the design appeared more balanced with a second mast. *Sea Swan*'s owner was not the only one who chose his boat for its looks.

Sails

Working sails did not come within the scope of the Suva survey, but, since many boats had sailed considerable distances under trade wind conditions, I discussed with the skippers the question of sail arrangements for down-wind sailing. Sixteen boats had twin jibs and/or genoas and every one of their skippers swore by them. Some of the twins were set flying or on the same stay with hanks alternating, although a few boats had twin forestays for this very reason. Some skippers mentioned that poled out twin jibs were easier on their self-steering, enabling it to be better balanced and work less, especially when running with a heavy following sea. For running down-wind, two of the schooners used a square sail set on a yard, generally in winds of over twenty knots.

Only five of the 62 boats were fitted with furling headsails, and their owners were satisfied with this arrangement, although each one pointed out that they seldom reef their headsail in this way and only use it for furling. Three of these five also had a staysail, which would explain why they did not use their jib furling gear for reefing. Twenty of the boats surveyed had spinnakers in their lockers, where they seemed to remain most of the time. Asked to rate the spinnaker as a cruising sail, only four out of twenty skippers came out in its favour. Overall, the spinnaker got a low average rating, 4·2.

When the twelve circumnavigators were asked to outline features of their planned or hypothetical next boat, only two gave a definite yes to jib furling gear, four gave it the thumbs down, while the rest were undecided and may still consider this arrangement.

From these circumnavigators I was able to get some idea of the wear and tear on sails. Disregarding one boat, which left and returned with no less than 21 sails, the average boat left with 7 sails and returned with 6·5. Several boats replaced sails en route, usually the main and genoa, and their estimated mileage per sail worked out at an average of 30,000 miles, although this does not mean that the particular sail was actually used for all those miles. Of course the state of the sails on setting out was a critical factor, but a few boats completed their circumnavigations with all the same sails that they had set off with, including *Lou IV* who, with 46,000 miles in

4½ years, had made one of the longest voyages on one suit of seven sails.

The longevity of the sails depends on two main factors. First, the quality of the material and workmanship, and secondly the care taken looking after the sails. Continuous exposure to the tropical sun exerts a heavy toll on any sail, although certain brands and colours of synthetic materials appear to be more resistant to heat and ultraviolet rays than others. More often than not it is the stitching that disintegrates long before the material itself, and several boats had their sails restitched in New Zealand halfway through their voyage. Another boat which completed her 50,000 mile world voyage, virtually with all her original sails, even if repeatedly repaired, was the French yawl *Calao*. Her skipper, Erick Bouteleux, preferred to have his sails made of much heavier cloth than that usually recommended by sailmakers. *Calao*'s heavy sails stood up very well to six years of continuous cruising, even if Erick had to fall back on his 1000 sq ft spinnaker and mizzen staysail whenever the winds got too light.

Taking good care of sails can undoubtedly prolong their lives considerably. Herbert and Ilse Gieseking of *Lou IV*, who returned home with the same sails they had set out with, were always meticulous about putting on the sail covers the minute they dropped anchor, folding away carefully the sails which were not in use and giving all sails a rinse ashore with fresh water whenever possible.

Despite careful attention and good materials, sails will eventually wear out and it is only the lucky few who manage to arrive home after a world cruise with their original sails. When sails need replacing during a cruise, there are three options open to the skipper, to have new sails made locally, to order them elsewhere and fly them in, or to make the sails himself. Although a number of cruising boats carry a sewing machine on board, these are rarely used for actual sailmaking, but rather for sail repairs, the making of awnings and dodgers, loose covers, etc. Sailmaking is one of the few jobs, which cruising people prefer to leave to the professionals.

With the world wide expansion of boating and sailing, there are now sailmakers to be found in all major centres along the cruising routes of the world. New Zealand and Australia are two countries where the sails made locally are of the same standard as those made in Europe and North America, in fact some of the old established sailmakers have their own branches in these countries. Hong Kong has also gained an international reputation for sailmaking of a good quality at a reasonable price and there are several sailmakers who are prompt at dispatching sails to every part of the globe. Some skippers still prefer to have their sails made by their original lofts, especially as these lofts usually hold the sail plans, which makes ordering easier. The sailmaker will generally arrange the air freighting or shipping of the finished sails. In most countries, if the shipment is marked *In Transit*, the owner can redeem them from Customs without paying duty. This may have to be arranged through a local shipping agent. However in a few countries, goods cannot be imported duty free and the skipper would be well advised to make his enquiries at Customs before placing an order overseas. It is also worth choosing a port convenient to an international airport as, in some countries, Customs insist that the goods are accompanied by an officer until they are on board. These general points apply also to the import of any replacement parts for a cruising boat.

Construction Material

As in the case of their rig, skippers were very precise when asked to give a rating to the material of their boat's construction. Over half of the boats (53 per cent) were of fibreglass, a material which received the overall average rating of 9; the four ferrocement boats also got the same rating. Metal boats were rated the highest, each of the five steel boats being rated the maximum 10, as was the only light alloy hull. As might be expected in tropical waters, wood received the lowest rating; the fifteen boats (24 per cent) were given an average rating of 7·9, whereas the four plywood boats were rated even lower at 5·6. In the few instances where the hull was sheathed, being made either from solid wood or ply, the material attracted higher marks from the owners. I later learned that one of the plywood boats, the 46 ft trimaran *Antigone*, who had rated his construction material very low and complained to me about it, did in fact run into trouble after leaving Suva on the passage to New Zealand. The hulls were in danger of breaking up and the boat had to put into New Caledonia for major emergency repair.

Among the twelve circumnavigators surveyed, four boats were wooden, while the rest were of fibreglass, one being fibreglass on ply. I had not asked their opinion on the construction material of their present boats, but when I questioned them on their future plans and boats, an interesting point emerged. There was a definite changeover to metal hulls. Either by choice or from financial considerations four crews were keeping their present boats. Out of the rest, four were changing to steel and one had his hopes pinned on light alloy. Even so, one of those keeping his present wooden boat told me that his hypothetical ideal boat would be a steel version of his present boat, but increased in size to 38–40 ft. Not all the future plans of the circumnavigators were just pipe dreams as two of them have already purchased or nearly completed their new steel boats.

Power

ENGINES

The wind has long ceased to be the only energy source used in cruising and most of the boats I came across had auxiliary engines. All of the circumnavigators had inboard diesel engines, but these were generally little used except when entering and leaving port or motoring in the calmest of weathers. The majority of these twelve skippers estimated that they sailed 95 per cent of the time. Some of the smaller boats claimed to use their engines even less than this.

In the Cruising survey, only three out of fifty boats were engineless. This was by deliberate choice, although Albert Steele later fitted an engine in his *Peregrine*, for the sole purpose of pottering among the reef-infested waters of the Tongan archipelago.

In my Suva survey, two boats were engineless, also by choice, although both skippers agreed that life would have been easier *with* an engine. In this survey I asked for more details about the engines, and requested a rating. Of the sixty boats with engines, the two smallest boats had outboard motors, one boat had a petrol (gasoline) inboard engine, rated 0, and the remaining fifty-seven were all equipped with diesel engines. The overall reliability of the diesel engines was shown by the average rating of 8·8. Nevertheless, some makes were rated higher than others. This did not necessarily reflect the better quality of the engine in question, but often the availability of spare parts and the ease of getting repairs dealt with promptly.

Several owners complained at the difficulty of finding parts for their Volvo engines in the Pacific, and this complaint was borne out by the low rating of 7·04 given to the twelve Volvo engines surveyed. The eighteen Perkins engines (14 Perkins, 4 Westerbeke) received a better average rating of 9·53. Parts for these engines are relatively easy to find, as in many cases the same parts are used in heavy plant or truck engines, and these are available in most countries. For similar reasons, the five Ford engines were also rated high at an average of 8·9.

Herbert Gieseking, whose *Lou IV* has figured in all three surveys, suggests that people fitting out for a world cruise may well be advised to fit a marinised truck or industrial engine, for which it is always easier and cheaper to find spare parts. His new boat will be equipped with a 120 HP Ford.

When the fresh water pump on my own Perkins engine gave up the ghost in Tarawa lagoon in the Gilbert Islands, I was amazed to be handed a replacement off the shelf in the well equipped government store at Tarawa, so I know from personal experience the advantage of having an engine for which spares are readily available. Many boats carried a selection of essential spares for their engines. The minimum specified by various skippers included a head gasket, at least one complete injector, a belt for the alternator and impellers for the various pumps. Equally important was the recommended set of tools for the engine in question, a workshop manual and a diagram showing all part numbers.

BATTERIES AND ELECTRICS

It is evident that many skippers prefer to be able, if necessary, to start their engines by hand. For those engines which cannot be hand-started, a separate battery charging source was advisable, for the refusal of a diesel engine to start, often in an emergency, was rarely due to an internal fault, but more frequently to a flat battery. It can be dangerous to rely on being able to start the engine instantly and then find that it won't start; this is how at least two boats are known to have been lost in recent years in the Pacific. Many cruising boats now feature separate banks of batteries, one for general use, the other for the sole purpose of starting the engine. The two circuits can be separated either by a blocking diode or an isolating switch.

ENGINE SIZE

For cruising in Pacific waters most skippers were of the opinion that a sufficiently powerful engine was essential. Many passes into lagoons have strong outflowing currents, being on the leeward side of the islands; and a lot of them are too narrow for tacking. Not a single skipper complained about having *too much* power – the complaints came from those who felt that their engines were not powerful enough. This point was reflected by the circumnavigators, three of whom planned a more powerful engine in their next boat. Trying to find an answer to this problem, I calculated the ratio between engine power in HP and the length of the boat in feet; as the power increased at a faster rate with size, I subdivided the boats into three categories, up to 40 ft, 40–50 ft and over 50 ft.

Over half the boats (32) fell into the first category, being under 40 ft long, and the average ratio of horse power to length worked out at 0·8 HP per foot of length. The seventeen boats in the middle category showed an average ratio of 1·5, while the eight boats over 50 ft long had an average of 2·4. The overall consensus appeared to be that one horse power per foot of boat length was about enough, although for smaller boats this ratio could be slightly reduced.

On the question of fuel capacity, I found that the average forty five gallons carried on most boats over 35 ft in length seemed to be sufficient. Diesel fuel is available in all major ports and for passages where a lot of motoring was expected many skippers augmented their fuel tanks with jerrycans lashed on deck.

Generators

Even the simplest boat needs some electricity, although only half the boats surveyed had a large enough electricity consumption to warrant an auxiliary generator. Twelve of the bigger boats had inboard diesel generators, fifteen had portable petrol (gasoline) generators and two boats were equipped with solar panels, which were regarded as satisfactory even if rather expensive to install. One boat had a generator attached to its freewheeling shaft, while another had a hydrospinner; which was towed behind the boat. Most boats under 40 feet seemed satisfied to charge their batteries from the alternator or generator attached to their main engine. On most boats the main energy consumers were radios and refrigerators, although not all of the latter were of the electrical type.

Refrigeration

In the Suva survey less than half the boats (45 per cent) had refrigeration of some kind. Those fitted with a mechanical compressor were rated the highest at 9·4, while those with an electrical compressor were rated at 7·7, those running on paraffin (kerosene) at 7·5 and those on bottled gas at 6·3. In the case of freezers, the seventeen boats that had them (27 per cent of the total), rated those driven by mechanical compressors much higher at 9·3, than those with electrical compressors, rated 6·3. Generally, I found that a mechanical compressor attached to the main engine gave by far the best results and attracted the highest ratings from their users, as it supplied both the freezer and the fridge. On boats with electrical refrigeration, the main engine had to be run for approximately forty five minutes to one hour a day, with the added advantage of the batteries being charged at the same time.

Instrumentation

The unprecedented advance in electronics in recent years has enabled cruising boats to carry an entire range of the latest instruments, powerful radios, radar and satellite navigation equipment, although many navigators seem equally happy to get by with just the basic instruments.

RADIO

An increasing number of cruising boats carry radio transmitters on board and these fall into three broad categories, VHF radiotelephones, ship's transceivers commonly known as SSB sets, and amateur sets, also known as ham radio. For the long distance ocean voyager the VHF sets have a limited use as their transmitting range is restricted to 30–50 miles and therefore I did not include them in my survey.

The most popular type of radio transmitter was the amateur radios, 23 of the boats surveyed in Suva had one of these sets on board. Amateur radio communication has been a popular hobby with countless enthusiasts throughout the world since the early days of radio. By international agreement amateur operators can only transmit on certain frequencies and these frequencies are reserved for their use. Many yachtsmen have become enthusiastic radio amateurs and this is reflected in the high average rating of 9·35 given to these sets by their owners.

Seven boats had SSB transmitters on board and these were given an average rating of 5·6. SSB radios operate over a wide range of frequencies different to those operated by the amateurs. These sets cost much more than the standard amateur set and also use more power, two good reasons which limit their appeal to the average cruising boat. Its use in an emergency is the main reason why most people equip their boat with a radio; yet several skippers who owned both types of radio complained that on large tracts of the ocean no one seemed to listen to the emergency frequency 2·182 MHz any more, whereas an emergency call on one of the amateur frequencies never failed to raise a reply.

There are now many amateur maritime networks in operation throughout the world, keeping track of boats on passage, supplying them with the latest weather information and providing a link with the outside world in case of an emergency. The yachting grapevine has taken over the airwaves and an increasing number of cruising boats are now keeping in touch via the amateur wave bands. The Seven Seas Cruising Association, an international voyagers' club publishes an up to date list of the principal maritime networks. It can be obtained against a small fee from the SSCA, P.O. Box 2190, Covington, Louisiana 70434, USA.

Amateur radio is rapidly becoming the yachtsman's best friend at sea, while Al Huso of *Potpourri* went as far as describing an amateur set as the best safety measure to have on a boat. Unfortunately getting a license for a mobile unit is still difficult in a number of countries. Several skippers felt that one should be allowed to carry an amateur set on board, provided it was only used in real emergencies, and that a basic license should be accepted in such a case. Some smaller countries issue amateur radio licenses for non-residents for a minimal fee, helping those who try to circumvent the cumbersome and outdated regulations in their own countries, but who wish nevertheless to preserve a semblance of legality.

The situation among the twelve circumnavigators accurately reflects the way things are moving in the radio world on cruising boats. Two boats had no radio equipment at all, nine boats had VHF radio telephones, although some of these were used very little. Two boats also had SSB transceivers, which were used even less, while on the other hand the five amateur radio operators used their equipment extensively. All five amateurs kept in contact with amateurs on other boats, while three of them also kept regular schedules with land based stations.

NAVIGATION

The scope of the survey did not allow me to investigate every navigation instrument separately, so I only asked the skippers to name their most useful and least useful instruments. It was quite a surprise to hear the answers to the question 'What do you regard as your most useful navigation instrument apart from the compass?', as only 70 per cent mentioned the navigator's loyal friend, the sextant. The rest varied between the log (16 per cent), depth sounder (8 per cent), radar and Omega. Perhaps this order of priorities meant that the 30 per cent who did not seem to have much use for their sextant preferred to sail by dead reckoning. The large number of wreckings in the Pacific caused by erroneous navigation may bear out this assumption. At least one skipper did not hesitate at all in giving his bottle opener as his most useful instrument! As to the question concerning 'the least useful instrument', two skippers unhesitatingly replied 'my wife', the ladies in question being present on both occasions. Marital problems aside, RDF came out really poorly in this section, maybe because of the lack of useful beacons in the Pacific. Windspeed indicators and a host of other electronic instruments and gadgetry were rated equally low. Several keen radio amateurs listed their SSB set as their least useful instrument.

Complaints about the general unreliability of electronic instrumentation often came from skippers who knew about these things, such as Royal McInnes, who told me bitterly, 'If ever I equip a boat again, for every piece of electronic equipment, I would try and instal its mechanical equivalent.' I only wondered how Mac, a former electronics expert with McDonnel Douglas Aircraft Corporation, hoped to find a mechanical back-up for the eight radios he carried on board. Perhaps by using an extra-large loud-hailer.

The main problem is that the average person has little idea how to repair his electronic equipment if it does fail. If he is lucky he will come across Dana Crumb, whose boat *Whistler* is well endowed with electronic equipment, all in working order. Dana, a retired computer wizard from IBM, not only helps repair equipment for friends, but puts life back into outboard motors and generators on remote islands and even helped restore telephone communications that had broken down in part of Papua New Guinea.

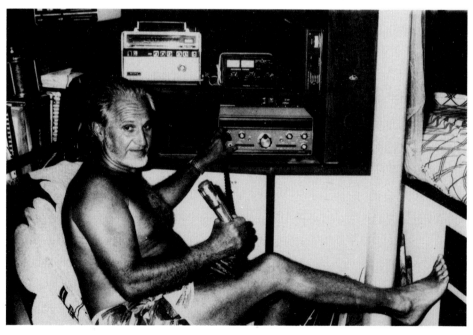

Amateur radio has gained enormous popularity among cruising people. The advances in electronics have brought small compact equipment within the reach of most people's pockets. Dana Crumb on *Whistler* keeps regular contact with many cruising friends.

Selfsteering

As all the boats surveyed had sailed considerable distances offshore, it was surprising that six of them had neither selfsteering gear nor autopilots. Among the remaining 56 boats, 42 (68 per cent) had some kind of windvane selfsteering, while 27 boats (44 per cent) had an automatic pilot. Fourteen boats had both selfsteering and autopilot, hence the percentage discrepancy. Of the total number of selfsteering devices, 29 were commercially made and were rated higher (average rating 8) then the 13 homemade ones (rated 6·7), although the home built gears attracted higher marks when they had been copied from proven models. Generally the well tried and proven models were given higher ratings by their owners. The most commonly used gear (7) was the UK made Aries, which got an average rating of 9·86. Of the five trimarans surveyed, three had selfsteering and their skippers were satisfied with their performance, giving them an average rating of 8.

All the twelve circumnavigators, which I surveyed later on, possessed selfsteering devices. Again, Aries was the most popular make (5 boats), with the Windpilot second (3 boats). Only two of the twelve left home with an automatic pilot, although another two added them en route.

Assessing the merits of a particular type of selfsteering device is a very subjective matter, as so much depends not just on the gear itself, but also on the sailing and handling characteristics of the boat in question, as well as on the skipper's skill in getting his boat perfectly trimmed and balanced. Best results were achieved by those able to fit a trim tab to their main rudder. The gears that incorporated a servoblade fared much better than the independent devices, which often proved to be under-powered in the boisterous sailing conditions encountered on some long ocean passages.

Because selfsteering devices are such an essential feature on any long distance cruising boat, I later made them the subject of a separate survey. In a sample of 50 cruising boats, 36 had selfsteering gears, 9 of which were homemade, the remaining 27 being stock designs. As in the previous survey, the largest number of these gears (12) were made by Aries, with an additional two having Monitor gears, which is an American design, almost identical to the Aries. The remaining 13 were divided among 10 different makes, so a comparison between the various makes was impractical. Hydrovane was another UK-made gear also praised by its two owners, one of whom was a singlehander who used the gear even to sail him out of port. The Swedish-made Sailomat also scored highly on all points of sailing, its only disadvantage being its very high price, whereas in the case of the cheaper French-made Plastimo, its owner wished the manufacturers had

Circumnavigator Herbert Gieseking of *Lou IV* gave a top rating to his Windpilot selfsteering device.

made it 25 per cent larger and stronger. Overall, the 36 gears had been used on average 16,200 miles per boat, two years being the average time they had been in use, as several boats had only fitted selfsteering gear *after* the start of their voyages.

As in the Suva survey, the homemade gears were rated lower at 7·6, than the commercially built gears at 9·1, this rating being both for strength and reliability. The structural strength of the equipment was an essential factor mentioned by several skippers, who also suggested to other voyagers to bear this important point in mind, especially those planning longer voyages. Having noted the frequent breakdowns and poorer performances of the homemade gears, I am tempted to agree with Jay Becker of *Jocelyn*, who advised those considering installing a selfsteering device on their boats, 'Go out and buy the strongest and best gear that is suited for your boat. Don't mess about with selfmade things or you will regret it later, when it actually matters.'

The skippers also rated the performance of their gears on various points of sailing, but no real pattern emerged from this data, since the success of a

The functional stern of 36 ft double-ended *Hero* offers not only protection to the Sailomat selfsteering gear, but also provides stowage for other equipment.

particular gear depends not only on its inherent quality but also on the sailing and steering characteristics of the boat in question. As expected, all gears performed well when the boats were closehauled, whereas their ratings differed widely when broadreaching or running. Invariably, the boats running with twin jibs rated their selfsteering gears higher than when running with other sails.

Among the nineteen gears which relied on a servoblade to provide additional force, on eleven boats the lines were led from the vane to the tiller, while on the remaining eight boats the steering wheel was fitted with a special drum to take the selfsteering lines. The latter arrangement was generally satisfactory, but in a few instances the skippers did mention that their boats appeared slower to respond, and for this reason, three skippers of boats with wheel steering had auxiliary tillers fitted to take the selfsteering lines. Wheel drums fitted to mechanically driven steering systems consistently gave better results than those fitted to hydraulic ones.

Because of the hard use the gears were submitted to, several of the stock designs had to be strengthened or slightly modified. Nearly half the gears broke at some point, although in most cases could be repaired immediately. Several skippers admitted that the breakages were probably the result of poor maintenance, which was not always the fault of the users. Some manufacturers ignore this aspect and give little or no advice regarding the proper care and maintenance of the gears. Another point raised by the skippers was the disadvantage of having the auxiliary rudder or servoblade permanently in the water, as not all makes have a way of lifting these up when not in use. Especially at anchor such gears were in danger of being hit and damaged by the dinghy, or were just noisy, while the wooden blade of a Mark II had been attacked by teredo worms during its permanent immersion.

Hardly any of the gears rated well in light airs and several skippers pointed out that with most gears there is no easy answer to that: one either had to steer by hand or opt for an automatic pilot. This is perhaps why an increasing number of cruising boats are doubling up their selfsteering capabilities by equipping themselves with an autopilot as well as a mechanical self-steering gear.

Ground Tackle

As docking facilities outside of Europe and North America are extremely limited, the boats surveyed spent most of their time in port at anchor. Ground tackle was therefore another major point of discussion. The majority of boats (85 per cent) used chain only with their main anchor; nine boats used chain and line. To qualify as 'chain only', the boat in question had to have at least 100 feet of chain on board, although I found that most boats carried twice that amount or even more. As for the strength of the chain, I found that all boats under 35 ft in length used $\frac{5}{16}$ in chain, while most of the boats between 35 and 45 ft used $\frac{3}{8}$ in chain, and the larger boats heavier still.

For extended cruising chain appears to have several advantages over line, not least of which is its better durability. The use of a powerful and reliable windlass was highly recommended by many and in the case of some elderly crews, the investment in an electric windlass was wise.

As to the type of anchor used, 49 boats (79 per cent) preferred a CQR as their main anchor, giving this type of anchor an average rating of 9·1. The eleven boats using Danforth anchors as their main anchor rated its holding power at 8·8, although I found that the Danforth anchors used were often much heavier than generally recommended for the size of boat in question; two anchors were over 200 lbs. Often I found that the CQR anchors were also heavier than is commonly regarded as necessary. Long distance voyagers anchoring in unknown anchorages obviously want to sleep well at night. I also found that all boats had at least one spare anchor of sufficient weight to be used as a main anchor in an emergency.

By working out the ratio between anchor weight in pounds and boat length in feet for each boat and then balancing out the results, I arrived at the average figure of 1·17 (e.g. 30 ft boat, 35 lbs anchor). A rough and ready rule of one pound of anchor for each foot of boat length was indicated.

Tenders

Loyalties were fairly evenly divided between hard dinghies (wood or fibreglass) and inflatables. I asked the skippers to rate their dinghy from the point of view of an overall yacht tender. The 43 hard dinghies received an average rating of 8·6 as opposed to the 7·8 rating given to the 40 inflatables. (Several boats had more than one, many larger boats carrying both a hard dinghy and an inflatable.) The smaller boats were often forced to choose a one-and-only inflatable because of the problem of space.

While many of the boats had more than one dinghy on board, only 40 out of the 62 boats surveyed had an inflatable liferaft available, the remaining skippers claiming to have other arrangements in case of an emergency. It was interesting to note that all the European boats had liferafts, except for one Frenchman who vowed he would never abandon his steel boat, but would go down with her if it came to that. Actually four skippers told me that they had no intention whatsoever of abandoning their boats. Of the remainder, ten had made provision to use their inflatable dinghies, seven keeping them permanently inflated on deck, while the other three had them fitted with CO_2 bottles for rapid inflation. Six of those who had hard dinghies but no liferafts, intended to use these if disaster struck, three of the tenders being provided with mast and sail for this purpose. Two other crews without a liferaft relied on Hawaiian paddling canoes for their rescue, which were lashed on deck and could be easily launched if necessary.

The owners of the liferafts were generous in allowing two raft places per crew member. This overall ratio of 2:1 certainly made sense considering the restricted space inside a liferaft and the length of time one might have to spend there before being rescued. It did appear that there was a trend to preferring a manoeuvrable dinghy to an inflatable liferaft. A rigid sailing dinghy with sufficient buoyancy to make it unsinkable was often regarded as the best means of getting somewhere if the boat was abandoned. This may be the reason why several companies manufacturing inflatable dinghies and liferafts now have introduced means of sailing them.

Conclusion

To abandon a boat, though, one first has to have it and it did not take me long to realise that in most cases it was the financial aspect that determined the type of boat selected, the size of the owner's pocket being the crucial factor. There may not even *be* a perfect cruising boat in the real sense of the word, as individual requirements differ so much. If one could attempt any consensus from all these surveys, the most contented skipper would appear to be the owner of a steel cutter around 35–40 ft long, equipped with an engine of about one horse power per foot length of boat. He would probably cook with bottled gas, have a refrigerator driven by a mechanical compressor and also an amateur radio. When anchoring he would use chain only with a 45 lb anchor. The basic instruments of compass, sextant and log would appear to satisfy most navigators' requirements, most electronic gear being generally considered unessential and a matter of personal preference. The surveys also showed that even if a particular skipper had not left on a voyage with such ideas, he may very well have come around to them after a long cruise. It is a view shared by Bruce MacDonald, whose personal motto is 'Keep it Simple', and who at the end of a circumnavigation on *Horizon* gave this advice:

'Do not fall for the equipment trap. You don't need a boatload of expensive electronics and other gear to have a safe, comfortable and enjoyable voyage. Establish your priorities. Determine what you can live without.'

Once those priorities are established, and assuming that one does not have the time, patience or money to build from scatch the cruising boat of one's dream, one should perhaps take the advice of Grant Neilson of *Iemanja.*

'Buy a boat that has already cruised, as most things you'll need will be already there, including many spares.'

Whatever the boat, and however it is equipped, these surveys confirmed my belief that it is the determination to go which matters most and that many people set off in the boat they just happen to own at the time, ideal or not. The motley collection of boats one meets sailing the oceans of the world may not be the ideal cruising boats, but their owners are the ones getting on with the cruising, not just dreaming or talking about it. For these crews the dream of cruising to faraway places has become reality.

ONE EXCELLENT BOAT – *HÄGAR THE HORRIBLE*

Only a handful of the boats I met in Suva came close to matching the ideals which emerged from my survey, although there was one outstanding example, which fulfilled virtually all the criteria of a perfect cruising boat. This was *Hägar the Horrible*, a 40 ft steel cutter from Sydney. Both on deck and below she was simple and functional. Her owner, Gunter Gross, had built her himself from a slightly modified design by the Australian designer Joe Adams.

A steel hull seemed the obvious choice for a boat built to cruise exten-

The steel cutter *Hägar the Horrible* from Sydney sailing out of Port Vila in the New Hebrides.

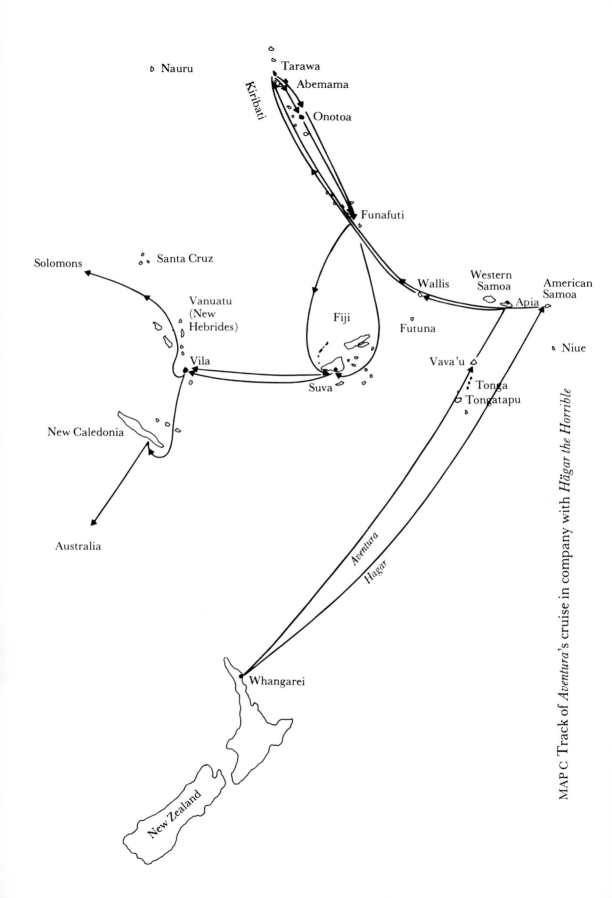

Nauru

Tarawa
Abemama
Kiribati
Onotoa

Funafuti

Solomons

Santa Cruz

Vanuatu
(New
Hebrides)

Fiji

Wallis

Western
Samoa

American
Samoa

Apia

Futuna

Niue

Vila

Suva

Vava'u

Tonga
Tongatapu

New Caledonia

Australia

Aventura

Hagar

Whangarei

New Zealand

MAP C Track of *Aventura*'s cruise in company with *Hägar the Horrible*

sively the reef strewn waters of the South Pacific. The high ratings given to metal as a construction material reflected the confidence associated with the strength of a metal hull. As all those who have sailed for any length of time in reef areas know only too well, however careful they are, sooner or later they may tangle with some coral heads. From this point of view alone, a metal hull has certain advantages over other materials. Being aware of the shortcomings of steel, Gunter had taken every conceivable precaution during construction to avoid any places where moisture could be trapped and cause rusting. The entire hull was easily inspected from the inside by removable floorboards and an ingenious modular furniture held in place by bolts. The steel was properly prepared and painted from the beginning.

Although of a fairly high aspect ratio, *Hägar* is easy to handle due to her cutter rig arrangement, with a selftending staysail controlled by a wishbone frame. The multichine hull is easily driven and performed well on all points of sailing, as I know only too well, being always left far behind whenever *Hägar* and my own *Aventura* sailed in company.

Gunter is an adventurer in the true sense of the word, something he proved the day I mentioned my intention to sail from New Zealand to the Independence celebrations in Tarawa, the island capital of the Gilbert Islands. We had spent the cyclone season together in Whangarei and although Gunter was planning to soon set sail for Tahiti once again, he changed his plans on the spot, undaunted by a detour of over 2,000 miles just to join in the festivities.

Although now Australian, Gunter was born in Germany and trained as a chef. Working on the Holland American Line he became convinced that sailing was his life, so with his excellent qualification he roamed the globe, trying to put enough money together to finance the boat of his dreams. From charter boats in the Caribbean to lumber camps in Canada and managing swish hotels in South Africa, it was finally as a cook at a bauxite mine in Australia that Gunter got enough cash together to have a 34 ft steel hull built, which he fitted out himself. Cruising up the Barrier reef, he soon found it was not a perfect blue water boat, so he decided to set about building the perfect boat with his own hands. Two years of hard work produced *Hägar the Horrible*.

Roving adventurer he may be, but Gunter is a meticulous skipper and his boat is always in tip top condition. He maintains his boat as he goes along, not allowing any job to be too long postponed. Six years of cruising have taken him 30,000 miles back and forth across the Pacific and he has realised his dream of making sailing his life. When he needs more money he stops to work, but one is more likely to find him as a boilermaker than a chef these days, as he has grown to enjoy working with metal as a medium.

Gunter Gross always keeps *Hägar* in good condition by doing maintenance work as it arises.

Although he usually has friends or crew on board, Gunter does sail *Hägar* singlehanded from time to time. I have certainly been impressed with the ease with which she handles and after spending several months in *Hägar*'s company, the boat certainly gets my vote as one of the nearest to perfect among the cruising boats I surveyed.

CHAPTER TWO

Living Afloat – the Practical and Administrative Aspects

Once a boat is chosen and equipped for a cruise and the conveniences of one's homeport left behind, problems of an entirely new nature start to loom over the horizon. Whether experienced or green, whether cruising on a shoestring or in great style, all long distance voyagers have to deal with certain practical matters such as the transfer of money overseas, forwarding mail, ordering spares and charts, and a host of other problems. These aspects are seldom mentioned when the beauty of blue water cruising is spoken of, yet their importance cannot be underestimated, for the success of many a cruise can be undermined by such apparently simple things that the skipper had failed to prepare for.

The Cruising Survey

Over a period of one year cruising in the Pacific from New Zealand to Tonga, Kiribati and Fiji, I interviewed every cruising boat I came across, trying to find out from their crews how they cope with these problems. As many of them were also sailors of considerable experience, I also asked them to make some practical suggestions to would-be voyagers. The 'Living Afloat' section of the survey ran to sixty questions concerning all practical matters of day to day cruising.

I started my work in New Zealand, where many boats which I had met previously in various corners of the Pacific were avoiding the cyclone season by passing the summer in the serene beauty of North Island's ports and coves. I had already interviewed some of the crews for my previous survey and I spent many a pleasant evening discussing these matters with my cruising colleagues, all of whom seemed to be as interested as myself in finding the best solutions to these practical problems.

In order to be sure of obtaining meaningful results, the boats surveyed had to fulfil two criteria. First, to have sailed a minimum of 5,000 miles away from base; and second, to have been cruising continuously for at least one year. As my data-gathering progressed I could afford to become more

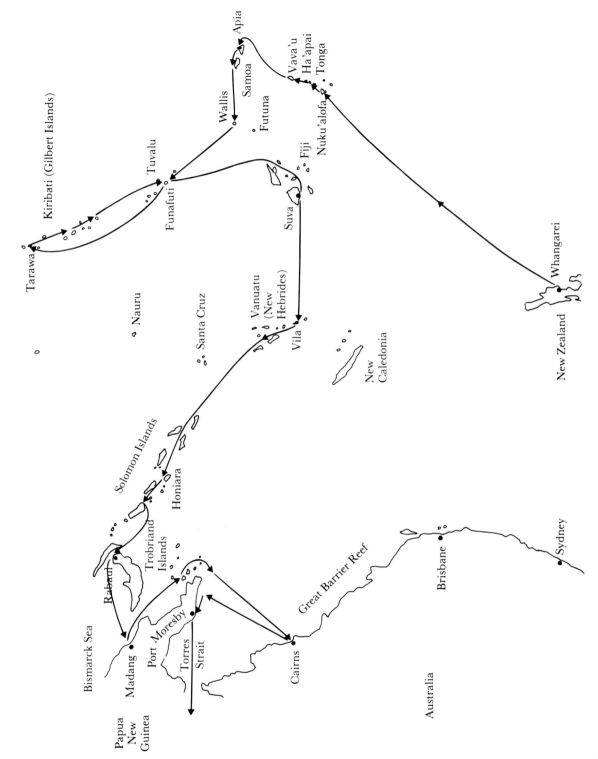

MAP D *Aventura*'s track while collecting data for the Cruising Survey

selective, trying whenever possible to talk to some of the long term voyagers, for whom cruising really is a way of life. The 50 boats included in the survey had covered a total of 1,190,000 miles on their present cruises, i.e. an average of 23,800 miles per boat, which is more than the circumference of the earth. In fact, the mileage would have been much higher if I had included in my calculation the total number of miles covered by the boat or skipper in question. Several of these had sailed many more miles in their long sailing careers, such as the Hiscocks on the various *Wanderers*, the Giesekings on *Lou I*, *II* and *III*, the Calmés on *Karak* and many others. *Merry Maiden* and *Diogenes* were on their second circumnavigation, while *Fortuna* and *Gambol* had both just completed their circumnavigations in Fiji.

Among the more experienced sailors interviewed were Georges and Hélène Calmé of *Karak*.

There were also two recent Cape Horners in this select lot, *Shangri-La*, claiming to be the first catamaran to make an east to west passage, and *Tehani III*. Jan Swerts, the Belgian singlehander of *Tehani III*, was unfortunately the only skipper I could not interview on his own boat as he had recently lost her on a reef in Fiji's treacherous Eastern Group.

For all the variety of boats and people encountered, the typical cruising boat turned out to be surprisingly similar to the findings of the survey I carried out the year before in Suva, 38 ft long with an average crew of 2·4. Sailing approximately 6,000 miles per year, the average time spent on the present cruise was four years. Out of the total of 50, 38 boats were crewed by a couple, either alone, or in eight cases accompanied by their children.

Finances

The financial aspect of world cruising is undoubtedly one of the most important factors to be considered before setting off. Unfortunately in today's age of permanent inflation, finances continue to be the single problem causing most concern to the majority of voyagers and the lack of finance a major reason for halting a cruise. Although I knew a number of crews quite well, I was gratified that out of the total number interviewed only one crew declined to give me exact figures, claiming that they had never even attempted to work out the approximate cost of cruising. The remaining 49 crews were all able to give me precise details on their budgeting, expenditure, source of income, etc. A simple statistical analysis based on these figures was then possible.

As the American dollar continues to be the most widely used international currency, I converted all costs quoted in other currencies into dollars. Also, as the data was gathered over a period of time and could have been grossly outdated by the time it appeared in print, I augmented the figures by $12\frac{1}{2}$ per cent per year, thus bringing all costs to the level of 1983. I feel that by applying an annual rate of world wide inflation of $12\frac{1}{2}$ per cent to these figures, the margin of errors has been reduced to a minimum.

CRUISING EXPENDITURE

To the crucial question of how much people spent during one year of cruising, I received a wide range of figures from $2,000 to $22,000 per boat per year, both of these boats having a crew of two. Such extremes however were rare, most of the figures quoted by the other crews being significantly grouped around the mean. To allow for the different numbers of crew, I calculated the average yearly cost per crew member, counting children under the age of ten as half, those over ten as a whole. This resulted in an average annual cost of cruising of $2,947 per person. By a different method of calculation, that of finding the mean cost per person per boat first and then averaging these results, I arrived at a figure of $3,406 per person per year. The two results are quite close to the annual cost per crew member of $3,000, which I regard as quite an adequate amount allowing one to cruise and live comfortably at today's prices, provided that the upkeep of the boat does not swallow up too much of this money. The figures quoted by each crew included all living expenses, maintenance and repair costs, even the buying of souvenirs, but did not include insurance premiums, which could be as high as $2,000 per year for boats cruising in areas considered as high risk by the insurance companies.

Two years later, when I carried out a survey among a dozen circum-navigators, these figures were confirmed by the new findings. Although the total cost of a world voyage varied widely, from a minimum of $8,000 to a maximum of $43,000, both voyages lasting three years, the average cost per circumnavigation worked out at $24,500. As the average length of these voyages was three years and nine months, the cost per boat per year amounted to $6,500. With an average crew of two, this figure comes very near to the one quoted above, of approximately $3,000 per person per year. Again these costs included all living expenses, maintenance and repairs, except in one case where an extra $15,000 was spent on a major refit of an older wooden boat. A few crews had also spent additional sums on regular flights home to visit their families, which are not incorporated. Although one would have expected that the longer a voyage the higher the cost, this was not the case. In fact, one of the longest voyages cost the least, its crew getting by with a budget of $200 per month. This was the lowest expenditure among the twelve circumnavigators.

Not only is diesel fuel continually rising in price, but in many countries is often dirty and has to be carefully filtered. Bill Stocks of *Kleena Kleene II* left home with a purpose-built filter, which separates both dirt and water out of fuel.

Although the above figures are only intended as a guideline, I would like to make some points for the benefit of those who take budgeting seriously. The runaway inflation of the last few years has affected most countries of the world, but life continues to be very reasonable by Western standards in most developing nations. On the other hand, there are a few spots which can quickly drain the resources of the unwary, such as Tahiti, and these are places which should be treated with care by those on a tight budget. Another factor to be kept in mind when planning a budget is the continual rise in the price of fuel. Also, as some of the developing countries are experiencing problems with their exports and are often short of foreign currency, fuel is becoming difficult to obtain in a few places, and is occasionally even simply unavailable for outsiders. Another item which can add considerably to expenditure is the cost of inland travel in the places visited.

BUDGETING

The material values and obsession with money that characterise western society were often among the main reasons why some of the sailors I met on my way around the world had left for a life at sea. This was perhaps the reason why more than half of those interviewed (28) did not operate a budget at all, just keeping an eye on expenditure in a vague way. Nevertheless practically all skippers, or more often their wives, were able to quote me the exact cost of their voyages. Georges Calmé of *Karak* reiterated the traditional principle of French good housekeeping when he said that, 'We try and live below our income like we have always done, which means that we try and economise all the time and in this way make ends meet.'

The people who kept a proper budget were generally those who were relying on a fixed monthly income, whether from pensions, investments or savings. Fourteen boats operated a monthly budget, which had to cover all expenditure. An additional two boats had a fixed budget for food alone and I found that only six boats had an itemised annual budget with allowances for living expenses, boat maintenance, insurance premiums, etc. The fourteen boats who operated a monthly budget kept this at an average of $512.50 per month, that is $6,150 per year. As in the previous examples, I have applied a $12\frac{1}{2}$ per cent per year adjustment to the figures quoted by those interviewed, so as to bring the costs as much as possible to the level of 1983. As all these boats who ran a monthly budget had an average crew of two the cost per person came out very close to the average figure of $3,000 per person per year indicated earlier.

On the subject of boat maintenance, only five skippers kept a separate

Not surprisingly one of the few skippers to keep an itemised budget was accountant Roger Morgan, whose cruising companion on *Fawn of Chichester* was Alice Simpson.

budget for this purpose alone. The average allowance for repairs and maintenance varied from 25 per cent to 50 per cent of the general budget expenditure and in several instances I was told that a capital replacement, such as a new dinghy or sails, also had to come out of this allowance. Several skippers who did not operate a special maintenance budget complained that the upkeep of their boats swallowed up more than half of their annual cost of cruising. This was particularly true in the case of several older wooden boats, which demanded continuous attention, but some of the largest boats in the survey, made of other materials than wood, were equally hard and costly to maintain.

Several owners told me that they aimed to keep their boat in tip top condition as a way of protecting their capital investment. Albert Fletcher of *Duen* fought a continuous battle to keep his traditional Norwegian fishing vessel in the best state possible, but he did not seem daunted by the mammoth task.

'It's the boat that eats the money, our personal needs don't compare with what the boat swallows. As long as we can keep up the boat we will hold on to it, otherwise we'd rather sell it. Many boats are neglected after the first

euphoria is over. I've seen it happen countless times. We protect our investment and our lives by keeping the boat in the best condition. A boat should
always be in a seaworthy condition.'

SOURCES OF INCOME

As the ages differed as widely as the financial resources of the crews, I
subdivided them into age groups, which enabled me not only to investigate
costing more closely, but also to analyse their source of income. In some
cases where the crew fell into different age groups, I included the boat
under the age of the skipper, especially as in some cases the ladies opted for
a lower age bracket, if they were near the borderline! As might be expected,
it was the youngest age group which spent the least amount of money. The
six crews which managed to cope with less than 1,400 dollars per person
per year, admitted that they often had a lean time. This was also the only
group to include boats which had left home with virtually no savings at all.
In some places en route, where jobs were available, these crews were forced
to stop and work in order to fund the continuation of their voyage.

TABLE 5. *Results of source of income questionnaire, Cruising Survey.*

Age	No. of boats	Average cost per person per year	Source of Income				
			savings only	savings & occasional work	pension &/or investment	no savings must work en route	charter
under 30	6	$1,383		2		3	1
30–40	24	$3,344	16	7	1		
40–50	8	$4,654	3	5			
50–60	9	$3,406	6		3		
over 60	3	$4,062		1	2		
Total	50		25	15	6	3	1

Looking at the table, it would appear that the most prosperous group
was the one in the 40–50 age bracket, but as this group also included some
of the crews with larger boats, who specifically mentioned much higher
maintenance and fuel bills, the average figures tend to give the wrong
impression. In practice, I found that in real terms the crews with more

money to spare were those in the 30–40 age group, who generally had kept the size of their boats in tune with their age, that is between 30–40 feet, being thus able to spend their money on other things than maintenance and fuel bills.

Herb Payson, the witty skipper of *Sea Foam*, summed up many people's feelings when he said. 'The biggest inhibition to cruising is not having enough money, then letting things go . . . It takes all the pleasure away, the lack of money, the shortage of funds to have repairs carried out by specialists when necessary. The voyage should not be undercapitalised.'

Herb's wife Nancy, who had been listening quietly to our conversation, added her own piece of advice for intending voyagers, 'Nevertheless, better do it on a shoestring than not at all.'

From what I was told, it appeared that exactly half the crews financed their voyages entirely from savings. An additional 15 crews did occasional work to replenish their funds in order to either extend their cruise or provide additional comforts. One of the skippers was financing his round the world cruise entirely by chartering and I found that at least five other boats relied heavily on taking paying crew or guests. This method of virtually selling berths on one's boat is becoming more and more a popular way of earning money while cruising. It may be an easy way of funding the continuation of a voyage, but the number of disgruntled and frustrated skippers who complained about their fare-paying crew members shows that what is easiest is not always the most pleasant.

What other possibilities of earning money underway are there? Generally, these fell into two categories, work ashore and work afloat. In spite of the restrictions imposed by most countries, hardly anyone who was willing to work failed to find some kind of employment, although often they had to look hard and be content with working illegally in unskilled jobs.

Stuart Clay of *Gambol*, who has worked his way around the world, earning money as he went along, had the following advice to give to others in a similar situation. 'Try and have some kind of income so as not to have to rely on work all the time, because often it is not easy to find. Also have some savings to fall back on if no work is available.' Nevertheless Stuart did manage to replenish the kitty throughout his six year long circumnavigation, perhaps because he was always ready to accept any kind of work that came his way.

In a better position were the people who had skills enabling them to find work on other boats, either on local craft or on other cruising boats, such as boatbuilding, sailmaking, carpentry, mechanical or electrical engineering. There were also a few who took their work with them wherever they went, freelance writers, jewellery makers and even a stock market speculator, who tried to keep in touch with his broker by telephone whenever he could. The medical profession was well represented among those interviewed and included several doctors and nurses. In a few places some of these were able to find temporary locum appointments, usually while local staff took their vacations. Ruth Abney, *Incognito*'s mate, is a qualified sailmaker and never seemed to be short of work. She was often seen stitching away at someone's damaged sail on the spacious floor of the Suva Yacht Club. 'If you have no regular income or savings, try and have a way of earning money as you go along,' she suggested.

A quite unusual and unexpected way of earning money cropped up during my stay in French Polynesia. Along with several other crews, I happened to be in Bora Bora exactly when the Italian film producer Dino de Laurentiis was desperately looking for extras for a new version of 'Hurricane', which was being filmed on what James Michener has described as the 'most beautiful island in the world.' As we all had to play the parts of American sailors in the 1920's, beards, moustaches and locks of hair fell under the ruthless shears of an Italian barber, but at least this sacrifice on the altar of art kept us all in beer for a long time to come. More work as film extras was forthcoming the following year on another film.

Earning money as a film extra is unfortunately a rare stroke of luck for the shortfunded world cruiser, but there are other ways of earning money en route. Sometimes it was not necessarily money that was earned, but the goodwill of local people, whether one managed to repair a faulty radio, a broken pump or outboard motor, or to stitch up a thumb split in two, as happened to Jean-Francois Delvaux, a radiologist from Paris, while cruising in Indonesia. Because cash still has limited usefulness in many of these remote places, it is just as well that the local goodwill is often translated into gifts of fruit, vegetables or even meat. Those who expect to run a tight budget during their world cruise should make sure that they have at least a good set of tools on board, so as to be able to do a job ashore if the occasion arises. Obviously those having specialised skills would be well advised to take the tools of their trade along with them.

CREDIT AND CASH TRANSFERS

One does not have to be a financial wizard to cope with money transfers, currency regulations and rates of exchange, and most people quickly learn to deal with all these things, when they are continuously changing the colour of their money. A few skippers told me that they carry all their funds in cash, either because they preferred this or usually because they came from countries with strict currency regulations and could not have money easily transferred overseas. The majority of boats (33) carried little ready cash and arranged for their funds to be transferred to a local bank along their route either by cable or airmail transfer. A practice highly recommended by several skippers on arrival in a port was to ask the largest of the local banks to telex their bank back home requesting the transfer of funds. This rarely took longer than 48 hours, and the transfer charges cost about ten dollars.

Among those interviewed, only two skippers relied on the now rather outdated system of letters of credit, which they found to be a satisfactory but expensive arrangement. Another skipper received his pension by international money order, which he found slow and unreliable. Fourteen crews kept their funds in travellers cheques of one of the major currencies, recommending these as they cost only 1 per cent of the total value to buy, but generally yielded between 3 and 5 per cent more on exchange than ordinary banknotes. An added advantage is that travellers cheques are replaced by the issuing bank if lost or stolen.

Currency regulations vary enormously from country to country. In some places when money arrives at the bank from overseas, this can be issued in travellers cheques of a major currency. In more restrictive countries the incoming funds may have to be converted into the local currency, which may not be freely reconverted when one leaves. In such places it is wise to only transfer sufficient funds to cover immediate needs.

It was also recommended that a certain amount of loose cash be carried, preferably US dollars in notes of smaller denominations. The mystic attraction of the 'greenback' is still going strong throughout the world, some shopkeepers will give a better price on goods for them, while in some remote places travellers cheques cannot be cashed at all, and out of banking hours there is usually a barman or shopkeeper to be found who will change some dollars into local currency.

In today's world of instant credit, it was not surprising to hear from several well travelled skippers that they had now changed over to drawing their funds by using their credit cards. American Express operates a world wide scheme, which enables the card holder to draw up to $1,000 in travellers cheques on demand against a personal cheque. No extra charge is made for this service, which is now available in many locations around the world. In smaller countries, the American Express representative is usually only found in the capital. A booklet listing all addresses is available free from American Express. Six of the boats carried American Express cards, mainly for this reason, while the twelve holders of other credit cards (10 Visa, 2 Access/Mastercharge) used these mainly for the occasional purchase. One can also draw cash on the Visa card, although some of those who had used this facility, found it rather difficult in remote places. Generally though, drawing cash on credit cards is becoming easier as their usage increases.

For those planning a long voyage it would be wise to obtain the various credit cards while still in permanent employment, as banks or credit companies may refuse to issue them later on, having little trust in the credit worthiness of sailors.

Similarly, for those intending to spend any length of time in Europe, it is advisable to open a checking or current account with one of the larger European banks, which automatically gives the account holder the possibility to draw limited amounts of cash at any bank displaying the Eurocheque sign. These can now be found not only in the remotest places in Europe, but also in North Africa and the Middle East, and even some banks in the Caribbean would cash a personal cheque accompanied by a Eurocheque card.

SHARING COSTS

Another topic of discussion with the fifty skippers was the financial arrangements they made with friends or crews joining their boats. Twenty boats had never had friends join them for any length of time, while twenty others expected their guests who joined them to share in all costs. Some skippers even specified that they would expect their cruising friends to foot the whole bill for drinks. The remaining ten boats made little difference between friends and paying crew, charging them a flat rate ranging from three to ten dollars per day. The skippers who applied the flat rate principle to their guests found that this caused less disagreement than the sharing of expenses.

Of the total number of boats surveyed, twenty eight never took on crew, being entirely self sufficient in this respect. As for those who took on crew, gone are the days when a deckhand could work his or her passage in return for his or her keep. All crews were expected to contribute towards costs to a larger or smaller degree. Eight boats generally took on crew only for longer passages and worked a shared expenses system. In these cases the crew were expected to help with the handling of the boat, cooking, washing up and taking watches. The skippers who preferred to charge a flat rate per day told me that they did not necessarily expect their crew to work, especially on the boats which charged a higher amount. On the other hand, one skipper who occasionally chartered his boat, while also having paying crew, always gave a share of the profit to these paying crew.

There was never any disagreement about the sharing of expenses on *Tarrawarra*. The crew, Steve, Tony, and Kim had been sailing together since they were teenagers.

Planning Ahead

MAINTENANCE SCHEDULES

Continuous cruising requires quite a bit of planning, yet I found that out of the 50 surveyed, only 21 planned to stop after a certain number of months to carry out basic maintenance work, hauling and antifouling. Fourteen skippers told me that they planned on stopping every twelve months, one boat every nine months, and six boats every six months. The remaining 29 boats carry out all necessary work as they go along, stopping only when convenient or absolutely necessary. Susan Hiscock complained about the tedious chore of maintaining their 50 ft steel *Wanderer IV*, which is probably one of the reasons why they gave her up in favour of *Wanderer V*:

'We plan our voyage around weather systems, not around maintenance requirements. Still, we seem to spend one third of our time on maintenance, one third on writing and only one third on going ashore.'

Often, hauling out for antifouling had to be planned around where a slipway was available, or at least a grid and a good tidal range. For larger boats with more than 6 ft draft, it was sometimes difficult to find a suitable place to haul. The majority of boats were only hauled out once a year or

Wanderer IV at anchor in Suva. Eric and Susan Hiscock are among the few people surveyed who have passed on their knowledge in writing.

The pilings on Nukulae island near Suva was a convenient place used by many crews to antifoul their boats between tides.

even less often than that, and because of this many skippers preferred to use a hard vinyl antifouling paint, which enabled them to scrub the bottom underwater as soon as the first slime or growth started forming.

In my previous survey in Suva, I had found that the average time since the last application of antifouling worked out at eleven months per boat, although hardly any brand of antifouling appeared to give satisfactory results after the initial six months under tropical conditions. Surprisingly enough the highest ratings were rarely given to the well known expensive brands, but often to copper rich paints, such as the ones used by the Navy. In two instances I was told of the excellent results achieved by using the special paint designed for submarines, but unfortunately this is not generally available. Good results were also reported with cheaper paints bought in tropical countries such as Venezuela, Costa Rica and Fiji and used by the local fishing boats. In the tropics where the danger from teredo worm is worst, boats with wooden hulls are most vulnerable, and more attention to both antifouling used, and the frequency it is applied, pays off.

SPARES AND REPAIRS

As well as the high cost in money and time of keeping a cruising boat in good running condition, most skippers emphasized the difficulty of obtaining even the simplest spares in some places. Because of this, many boats carried on board all essential spares. One skipper suggested that if this was not possible, at least have specification lists available to facilitate the ordering of spares. Dud Dewey, who had spent several years in restoring the schooner *Hawk* to her former beauty, knew what he was talking about when he gave the following piece of advice:

'Take every spare you feel you will need later on, as cruising with the problem of finding spares can be a nuisance, a trial. I carry twenty pounds of stainless steel nuts and bolts on my boat and I am continually supplying other boats who cannot find even such basic things in the South Pacific.'

Dud, an ex-USAF pilot, had discovered the Adams-designed *Hawk* in a sorry state of neglect in a Florida backwater. Formerly known as the *Seven Seas*, the fifty year old schooner had belonged among others to Errol Flynn, and President F. D. Roosevelt was another famous person who had sailed extensively on this perfect example of East Coast boatbuilding.

Finding the skilled man to carry out specialist repairs can often be even more difficult than finding the necessary spare. Many skippers complained about the unsatisfactory work carried out in some countries. Very often it became a matter of either getting on with the repair oneself or being stuck in some remote corner forever.

Nick Zeldenrust, of *Kemana*, an ex-officer in the Dutch Merchant Navy, who later emigrated to Canada, where he worked as a land surveyor in the middle of the North American continent, declared himself totally committed to the principle of self-help:

'Most of the worries on a boat are caused by maintenance. Before setting off, one should learn about electrical work, even take a course in diesel mechanics, which can be done by correspondence. You don't have to be all that good with your hands to be able to carry out simple repairs on your boat.'

The twelve circumnavigators whom I interviewed later encountered very few serious problems during their voyages, although by far the commonest breakdown was engine failure, which always seemed to occur in remote places where spares and repair facilities were difficult to come by. Ironically, these boats used their engines very little and according to their skippers, sailed an average of 95 per cent of the time. Maybe their engines failed just because they were used so infrequently. The other common failure was that of standing rigging, although all faulty rigging was discovered and repaired during routine checks in port. As well as essential engine parts, spare rigging wire and accessories seem high on the list of items to be carried by any boat sailing further afield.

While discussing the subject of repairs with the skippers, I also asked them if they could carry out underwater work on their boats. Those who were in doubt about what was expected of them, I asked the specific question if they could, for instance, remove a line fouled around their propeller. In the case of every boat, I was assured that there was a mask and snorkel available and also that there was somebody who could dive overboard in an emergency. In the few instances where the skipper could not dive himself, either the mate or another crew member could do it, if such an action became necessary. In fact, thirteen boats carried full air tanks on board, which were rarely used for diving, but were kept for such an emergency. Two boats carried Hookah compressors, which enabled the crew to either work underwater, rescue a fouled anchor or more usually keep the hull free from growth.

Insurance

The possibility of a major or minor catastrophe must be at the back of every seafarer's mind, whether it is falling seriously ill in a foreign port, losing a mast or even the boat itself. Due to the high cost of insurance premiums for world cruising, I found that out of fifty boats, only eight were fully insured, three were insured for total loss only, while two others carried insurance for third party claims only. Seven of the insured boats also carried insurance for gear and personal effects. Of the total number of boats less than a quarter (12) had taken out medical insurance for all crew members, whereas in the case of life insurance, fifteen men had their lives insured but only five women. This did not necessarily mean that the skippers regarded their lives to be more valuable than those of their wives, but simply because many men had taken out life insurance while still working ashore and had kept these going when they left home.

Even if not insured, most boats (38) had at least an allowance available for major repairs, replacement of vital equipment or medical expenses. Generally I was told that this allowance would come out of savings, although in ten cases a special fund has been set aside to cover just such an emergency. One skipper, who would not even consider insuring his boat, claiming that it would give him a false sense of security, had put aside enough money to buy another boat if he lost the present one. Two couples on two different boats carried with them valid undated air tickets, which would enable them to fly home in a medical emergency. At the other end of the resource scale, twelve boats did not have any reserve at all, only two of these being insured. For most of these crews even a minor mishap could put their cruise in jeopardy. It is one of the many calculated risks they take.

Mail

The receiving and forwarding of mail seems to cause more headaches to world voyagers than anything else. The stories of mail missed, lost, sent back or miraculously retrieved after several changes of address, never fail to crop up whenever cruising folk get together. General Delivery/Poste Restante continues to be the most widely used receiving address, although far from the most satisfactory. Asked to rate this service from one to ten, the skippers gave General Delivery an average rating of 7·6. A few people pointed out however that in the case of parcels or packets, the rating should have been much lower. Particularly poorly rated were the Post Offices in some Central American countries and in French Polynesia, where mail is only held for two weeks before being returned to sender. The next commonly used address was that of yacht clubs, which received a similar average rating of 7·6, some clubs being better than others in holding or even forwarding mail. Fourteen boats have also used Port Captains or Harbour Masters as a forwarding address and these were rated higher than clubs at an average 8·8, being particularly recommended in countries where post offices were not reliable (Bali), or would not hold General Delivery/Poste Restante mail (Mexico, Tahiti). Some of the boats also used embassies or banks to receive mail, although it was advisable to write first and ask for permission to use this service. The average rating given to banks and embassies for holding mail was 9, while American Express offices received a rating of 10 from the four crews, who used its mail holding service for cardholders. In all cases it was recommended that 'Hold for Arrival' and the name of the boat should appear in bold letters on the envelope. One can always find out via the cruising grapevine the addresses of the best places for receiving mail that lie ahead. This is proving to be yet another advantage of amateur radio, as messages can be passed on quickly and effortlessly to other boats and missed mail can be immediately dispatched to the next port of call.

Charts

Navigation charts are very hard to obtain outside major ports and because of this the majority of the boats had made some provision to overcome this difficulty. Seventeen boats left home with more or less all the charts needed for their intended voyage, while six skippers preferred to place orders with a chart agent in their own country as they went along. Just over half the boats (26) left home with some charts, usually for about half the voyage, relying afterwards on swapping or buying charts from other boats.

Some boats, though, leave home with even less than the bare minimum as Beverly Wilmoth told me smilingly over a cup of coffee on board *Aslan*:

'We left San Diego with only one chart on board, showing Hawaii as a tiny speck in the bottom corner. I sure don't know how we ever found it.'

Not only did they find Hawaii, but by the time I started work on this book, *Aslan* had already circled the globe and was back home in Texas. Beverly and Scott are already toying with the idea of setting off into the blue once again, but this time with rather more experience.

A few skippers made a point of asking the officers of freighters for their used charts, which were usually given away and often included the latest corrections. Generally when charts changed hands between boats, the going rate was slightly less than half of the official price. A few boats also kept a good supply of tracing paper on board to copy borrowed charts, or at least the sections of interest to them. The availability and cheapness of photocopying has also increased the amount of charts copied in this way. Although it is not strictly legal, it is becoming commonplace in areas where it is difficult to obtain charts. It was also pointed out by one skipper, that even if one did not have all the necessary charts, it was essential to have all pilot books on board, as a rough sketch plan could always be drawn from the instructions contained in the pilot, if one was faced with navigating through a particular area without charts.

Firearms

The regulations on firearms vary enormously from country to country and cause some problems for voyagers. Firearms are sometimes bonded on board, but more often are removed by the authorities for the duration of the boat's sojourn in port. Therefore I asked the skippers who carried firearms aboard to rate their presence on board as an overall plus or minus. Of the nineteen skippers who had firearms, only six regarded them as a plus, twelve as a minus, and one was undecided. The six owners who considered that the trouble involved owning a gun was justified, told me that they regarded a firearm as an essential deterrent and would not consider cruising without one.

Dogs on boats created various problems for their owners, who all had misgivings about keeping them on board.

Pets

Again, the regulations vary enormously from country to country, and quarantine requirements can be even more strictly applied than the firearm regulations. Of the thirteen boats who had pets, seven considered them a plus, four a minus and two were undecided. None of the four dogs on boats received a plus rating. Ilse Gieseking of *Lou IV* admitted that setting off on a trip around the world with a dog had been a major mistake, because their freedom of movement had been severely restricted in many countries because of their dog. 'Although animals can be very entertaining at sea, when in port they are a nuisance, because they have to stay on board. Despite our love for our poodle Joshi (named after Joshua Slocum), we would never again take a pet on a future voyage, so as to be more independent . . . but thinking about it, perhaps I wouldn't mind a cat . . .'

Cats seemed indeed to be more suitable boat pets, receiving a plus rating, while the only other pet, a gecko, was also awarded a plus.

Erick Bouteleux of *Calao* had at least one good reason to like their cat, when he said, 'Our kitten is a positive plus. Since acquiring it in the Marquesas, we've never had to buy any toys for our two kids.'

Erick would certainly have changed his plus rating if I had asked him the same question one month later, when he had to fight to save his boat from sinking in the vicinity of Futuna. Falling off a wave in rough weather, *Calao* had sprung a leak and was taking in a lot of water. The electrical bilge pump could not cope at all with the influx of water, so Erick cut the cooling intake hose and let the engine draw water straight from the bilge. Only then did he have a chance to look at the bilge pump, which he found to be completely clogged with cat's litter.

Hobbies

The last part of the survey dealt with the sports and hobbies enjoyed by these voyaging crews. Photography appeared to be the most common hobby, but although with only two exceptions, all boats had a camera on board, less than half of those interviewed attempted to record their voyage in a consistent fashion. Of those who took photographs, these were divided evenly between prints and slides, with only a few using black and white film. Thirteen crews also had Super 8 movie cameras and one was shooting on 16 mm film for commercial purposes.

Although seventeen boats had sailing dinghies or canoes, these were little used for sport; the boats using them most were those with children on board. Nor did other water-related sports seem to be much practised by the world voyagers. Four had surfboards and only two carried sailboards, although I noticed later than an increasing number had been bitten by the sailboarding bug. None of the crews water-skied and, although several boats had air tanks on board, only one had a compressor for filling them and took diving seriously. Two boats had small motorcycles in their fore-peak, which were used for exploring the interior of places visited and usually it was quite easy to obtain permission to land the motorbikes. The crew of one boat, being keen mountaineers, made cross country hikes wherever possible.

Gunter Gross of *Hägar* had an instant reply when I asked him what sports he practised.

'The only sport I am interested in is girls!'

On the question of fishing for food rather than as a sport, 47 skippers claimed that they often trolled a line when on passage, although about half of them were candid enough to admit that they rarely caught anything. Eighteen of the fishermen were keen enough to also try their luck with a hook and line while at anchor. Twenty eight boats had spearguns on board, although only a few of their owners were serious spearfishing enthusiasts.

Away from the supermarkets, a freshly caught fish makes a welcome change for dinner.

The Future

In every instance I concluded my interview with a set of questions concerning a hypothetical future voyage. In spite of the many difficulties and tribulations encountered, all fifty skippers stated that they would willingly undertake such a voyage again. Such a unanimously positive response came as a surprise after some of the remarks made by a few skippers during our discussions had led me to think that they had doubts about the wisdom of their decision to set off into the blue.

Purely on a practical level, thirty of the fifty skippers told me that they would be quite happy to undertake another voyage on their present boats or on something very similar and would allow a similar amount of money. The skippers of six of the larger boats would opt for something smaller if they had the choice, while fourteen skippers would prefer slightly larger boats than the ones they had at the moment. Only one skipper said that he would need less money, but that was provided the boat was smaller, while the remaining nineteen would like to be able to afford a more generous budget. Most of these stated quite clearly that most of all they would like to be free of the necessity of looking for work.

The lack of sufficient funds can seriously undermine the pleasures of a voyage, especially today when less and less things come free and where in certain countries the ownership of a yacht indicates a certain affluence. Among the circumnavigators planning a new voyage however, five would allow the same amount of money as before, increasing it perhaps to take account of inflation, while a similar number would try and augment their budget by 20 per cent in real terms. Jean-Francois Delvaux of *Alkinoos* advises anyone planning a long cruise to try and have a basic minimum of money before starting.

'One should have enough money for at least the first year of the voyage, because after one has sunk all money into a boat, one should not be forced to stop and work as soon as one has left on the cruise of one's dreams.'

These are then some of the considerations and problems encountered by those who have chosen cruising as a way of life. The overwhelming impression I gained from talking to such a wide variety of people was their general contentment with their present lives. The fact that some were affluent and others not, that they were young or old, married or single, with or without children seemed to make no difference at all. They all managed to cope somehow with the practical side of cruising.

GAMBOL'S UNPLANNED CIRCUMNAVIGATION

Some people plan their cruise with great care and detail, while others just

Gambol sailing slowly into Suva harbour at the end of a six year long circumnavigation.

let things happen. In Fiji, I came across Stuart Clay who was completing a circumnavigation he had not planned to make. He told me of the haphazard way this had come about and how, after six years of adventures, he had finally crossed his outward track.

A farmer from Tipuki in New Zealand, Stuart had always been a sailing man, and most weekends would leave his cattle and sheep to go sailing. He had owned a variety of boats, but decided that his eighth and largest, *Gambol*, was just the job to take him farther afield, so he gave up farming and entered *Gambol* for the Auckland to Suva race. He finished in the middle of the fleet, but was happy with his new boat, a sturdy 37 footer, built of strip plank sheathed in fibreglass, so he decided to carry on cruising for a while. One of his crew also chose to stay and the two men spent ten months exploring the many islands of the Fijian archipelago.

Instead of returning home, they sailed via the New Hebrides and New Caledonia to Brisbane, arriving only two days before the great floods that struck that area. Concerned about his uninsured boat, Stuart arranged to have *Gambol* taken out onto the relatively dry shore, but even so the waters

MAP E Track of *Gambol*'s Circumnavigation

Darwin

Indonesia

Capetown

Ascension

St. Helena

Virgin Islands

Panama

Marquesas

Tahiti

Fiji

New Caledonia

New Zealand

rose over the banks, threatening to float her out of the improvised cradle.

When it was all over, Stuart entered *Gambol* in the Brisbane to Gladstone race, again crossing the finishing line in the middle of the fleet. By now both skipper and crew were broke, so they sailed on to Townsville and worked for nearly a year as deckhands on a dredge to replenish the kitty. Partly cruising and stopping to work periodically, Stuart made his way up inside the Great Barrier Reef to Cooktown, where his crew opted for life ashore. He found an Australian crew and sailed on to Darwin, where there was plenty of work and money to be made, rebuilding the town devastated by a cyclone that had hit the previous Christmas.

Soon *Gambol* was on the move again, sailing across from Darwin to cruise the Indonesian archipelago from Timor to Bali. Planning however is not one of Stuart's stronger points, so he found he was cruising in the wrong season with the North West monsoon in full swing. When the mainsail tore to shreds and the engine blew up, he realised he couldn't carry on and headed back to Darwin. It was back to laying bricks until a new mainsail and engine were paid for.

Having put *Gambol* back into good shape, Stuart took on a new crew and set sail across the Indian Ocean. It was easier to keep on going west then to head back home to windward across the notorious Tasman Sea. In Mauritius, Stuart met a South African businessman, who among other things told him to look out for his daughter in Durban. By chance Stuart ran into her the very first day he was ashore and that was the end of male crews on board *Gambol*. Pamela Church joined the cruise in South Africa, has been with Stuart ever since, although now she is Mrs Clay.

In March 1977, Stuart and Pamela left Capetown bound for the Caribbean. They called in at St Helena, but disaster nearly struck on the next leg to Ascension. All day long they had been sailing among a large school of whales, who seemed happy to keep them company, gamboling around the boat, sounding and surfacing near them. Night fell, a dark night, and *Gambol* was running along swiftly doing seven knots with main and boomed genoa wing and wing. Stuart came on watch at midnight and took over the wheel. A few minutes later there was a loud thump and the boat came to an abrupt halt, then she put her nose down, came up, and seconds later was moving again. A big bang like a retort followed, then absolute quiet. The impact had been sudden but soft, so Stuart knew instantly that they had not hit a log, yet the shock made the engine covers and floor boards shoot up into the air. On inspection, Stuart found no structural damage to *Gambol*, only a slight leak in the forward section near to the head. He is certain that they had hit a whale and that the second bang was caused by the whale sounding in fright and hitting them with its tail. Checking the hull later on, he found a few cracks in the fibreglass sheathing and a cracked plank, but nothing serious. Stuart still thanks his lucky star to have been in a strongly built boat and to have escaped with just 'a hell of a fright.'

The rest of their trip to Barbados was uneventful, but soon after arrival they made straight for St Thomas in the Virgin Islands to look for work, as Stuart was flat broke once again. 'It is the story of my life.'

They both found jobs with the big charter boats, painting and varnishing for four dollars a day, then Stuart landed a job as a skipper with the bareboat charter fleet based on Tortola in the British Virgin Islands. It was a sweet job with little work, briefing people on the bareboats they were going to charter. The same company, CSY, later appointed Stuart instructor in the local sailing school. Twenty months were spent there, Pamela and Stuart enjoying every moment of it. Work had not always been so pleasant and neither had it been easy to find on his way around the globe. Having left home with only a few months' cruise in mind, not years as it turned out, Stuart had been obliged to work as he went along to finance his cruising.

Eventually he got itchy feet again, so in 1979 he left the Virgin Islands, set sail for Panama and the wide Pacific. In Suva, Stuart completed the 45,000 mile long circumnavigation, that he had never planned, but then planning is not exactly the kind of stuff that men like Stuart are made of. Still, I could not resist asking him about his future plans. He recounted how he hoped to set off again, but would like to look for a larger boat, around 50 ft, large enough to take paying passengers, who would finance the cruise. The guests would get food, accommodation and a chance to see the world, while Stuart would not have to run around looking for work ashore. Ideally his next boat would be steel and I am sure he had the experience with the whale in the back of his mind when he specified that.

Stuart may not always plan, but this time he certainly kept to his ideas, for two years later he bought the Hiscocks' *Wanderer IV*, a 50 ft steel ketch, with which the Clays are now cruising the South Pacific.

DUEN'S CONVERSION FOR WORLD CRUISING

Graceful and striking, all eyes turn towards her as *Duen* sails into an anchorage. Gaff-rigged, top masts, and jibs set flying, *Duen* is a ship run and rigged as a sailing boat from the last century. Behind the beauty lies a tale of hard work and a continuing heavy load of maintenance, for keeping up this kind of timber vessel requires a rare dedication. Not every antique

Many years of hard work have transformed *Duen* from a shabby fishing vessel to a stylish sailing craft.

boat has been lucky enough to find just such dedicated owners as Albert and Dottie Fletcher.

Duen was quite different, a scruffy fishing vessel of uncertain years, when the Fletchers first set eyes on her in 1971 in a small port in Norway. It was Albert's romantic imagination that looked past the disused fishing gear, derelict hydraulic piping, rust, grease and oil and could already picture in his mind's eye the promised beauty of *Duen*. The 50 ft hull was solid and had been well cared for and with her double ended traditional lines, adapted to the rough conditions of the North Sea, she promised to become a sea-kindly cruising boat. So they bought her.

If Dottie had inspected the engine room, the story might have been different, for *Duen* was powered by an ancient Rapp one cylinder semi-diesel engine with a one ton flywheel, promptly nicknamed Rapp the Monster. It had to be started with a compressed air bottle and every hour on the hour seventeen holes had to be oiled, twelve grease cups turned and five wicks filled, a not very pleasant task at sea in the dark, smelly, hot engine room.

For eighteen months in Norway, the Fletchers worked solidly, 12 to 18 hours a day, gutting her, tearing out the old equipment and turning her slowly into the cruising boat they had dreamed of. The strength of the 50 ft hull, with a beam of 18 ft and a draft of 8 ft was impressive. The 9 by 9 inch frames were only seven inches apart, the two inch pitch pine outer hull being held together by four double sets of stringers fastened entirely by trunnels. In the cold winter they worked on the interior and in the warmer weather on the spars and rigging. They kept the Norwegian style pilot house and first set sail with *Duen* as a gaff rigged ketch with two short masts. Sailing alone and not being very experienced sailors, they were glad of the short rig. They learned as they went along, coast hopping southwards from Norway in search of warmer weather.

After a pleasant time in the Mediterranean and now more confident in their navigation and seamanship, they prepared to cross the Atlantic and take *Duen* back home to California. In the Caribbean however they lost the desire to rush; cruising had become a way of life and *Duen* their home. Joined by some of their family, they successfully chartered and spent several years in the Caribbean.

Albert then carried out the first of *Duen*'s transformations. Rapp the Monster was replaced and the pilot house dismantled, as it provided too much windage. With more space on deck, Albert could lengthen the boom and gaff and he also increased the sail area with a topmast. All the new spars he adzed out himself on the beach at Bequia.

When they finally got to California, Albert set about the third and final conversion for *Duen*. Now he had the experience and knowledge, he knew exactly what to do to turn her into a fine sailing vessel. In nearly a year of hard work Albert designed and made all the new spars, metal work and rigging. Then the Fletcher's set out across the Pacific in *Duen* as she is now, her varnished hull gleaming, a ketch with taller rig and jibs flying to the long bowsprit.

As might be expected for the owners of such a distinctive vessel, the Fletchers are not without character either. Albert is a burly Californian with a bushy black beard, tattooed arms and describes himself as a compulsive tool collector. Dottie, with her twinkling eyes, seems always to be laughing and I was quite surprised to find out that the young lad coiling ropes on deck was not her son but her grandson. *Duen* has often cruised for long periods with three generations on board and keeping the happy atmosphere on board ship owes much to Dottie's sense of humour.

Three generations make up *Duen*'s crew.

Maintaining *Duen* is a time-consuming and costly business, the boat swallowing up far more money than Albert and Dottie ever spend on themselves. If they cannot afford to keep her going, Albert would prefer to sell *Duen*, than to let her deteriorate. To help with the maintenance bills, the Fletchers take on paying crew and charter when they can. When I last saw them in Australia, they were delighted to be doing a television film sailing up the Great Barrier Reef. Everything helps to keep *Duen* going, although knowing Albert's talents and capacity for hard work, I am sure that *Duen* is in no danger of ever being neglected and she will continue to grace the oceans as a reminder of the past glory of sail.

CHAPTER THREE

Aspects of Seamanship

Boat designs, materials, rigs and instruments have radically changed over the years, and even some old established concepts of seamanship have come under scrutiny. The sea, however, is unchanging and still challenges the ocean voyager. In an attempt to find out if the techniques of dealing with these challenges have also changed or remained the same, I discussed these matters with the 50 seasoned sailors of my second survey, tapping their wealth of knowledge, acquired by first-hand experience. See page 165 for the details of boats and crews concerned.

The combined experience of the fifty long distance skippers, whom I interviewed personally over a period of time, was indeed considerable, yet only one or two of them have passed on their knowledge in writing. Susan and Eric Hiscock fall into a category of their own, with three and a half circumnavigations and over 200,000 miles to their credit, while Mike Bales of *Jellicle*, the smallest boat in the survey, has spent the last twenty years roaming the oceans of the world in his simple Folkboat. Some of the boats were even more famous than their present owners, like the fifty year old staysail schooner *Hawk*, previously the *Seven Seas*, once sailed by Errol Flynn and President F. D. Roosevelt; *Orplid*, formerly the *Hamburg VI*, a training ship for German Navy cadets, sadly lost since then on the Great Barrier Reef; *Peregrine*, the pre-war Fastnet racer skippered by the old salt Albert Steele; or aging *Fortuna*, with seven Sydney to Hobart races and two circumnavigations in her logbook.

My questions covered certain aspects of seamanship and the day to day running of the ship, but I also tried to find out from these experienced sailors how they dealt with heavy weather, various emergencies and other problems at sea.

Coping with Heavy Weather

Heavy weather tactics formed the core of the survey and I asked each skipper when and how he hove to, at what force of wind he would consider laying a-hull or running under bare poles.

Depending on the direction of the wind and having sufficient searoom, most skippers specified that they would carry on sailing in winds up to and including Force 7. With a wind forward of the beam or with land too close for comfort to leeward, most boats would heave to when the wind reached Force 6. Several skippers specified that they hove to not only when the weather deteriorated, but also to slow down, to await daylight for a land-fall, or in the case of a singlehander without selfsteering, just to rest.

Obviously the techniques of heaving to under sail depended very much on the characteristics and attitude of each boat, as well as on the rig. Thirteen skippers told me that they preferred heaving to under mainsail alone, either full when the wind was not too strong, or reefed. On another ten boats a small foresail was used in combination with the mainsail. Seven ketches usually hove to under a small foresail and mizzen, often reefing the mizzen. Even the skippers who did not rate a ketch too highly as a cruising rig, considered a mizzen sail to be an advantage when heaving to in heavy weather, as it was much easier to deal with than the mainsail. The skipper of one ketch who once hove to under deeply reefed mainsail in extremely rough conditions, found that the solid water breaking over the boat did not have sufficient room to run off under the main boom. He changed to stay-

When it comes to heavy weather, Kiwi circumnavigator Tony Ray of *Ben Gunn* is among the increasing number of skippers whose preferred tactic is dropping all sail and laying a-hull.

sail and reefed mizzen, which immediately improved the situation. The skippers of two boats chose to heave to under foresail alone, while one ketch normally hove to under mizzen alone and one schooner under jib and fore-staysail. The skippers of seven boats had never or rarely hove to under sail, going straight to laying a-hull when conditions deteriorated. Tony Ray, who sailed around the world on *Ben Gunn*, told me that being worried about breaking the large windows on the 29 ft Herreshoff sloop, they stopped heaving to and preferred laying a-hull when the weather deteriorated, reducing the amount of water breaking over the boat when lying in this way.

When hove to under a backed foresail and reefed mainsail, the boat continues to move ahead, although the foresail tries to counteract this. In strong winds this forward movement may cause heavy water to break over the boat and this is when most skippers would consider dropping all sail and either lying a-hull or running before the weather. When lying a-hull most boats take up a position with the wind and waves abeam, while drifting slowly to leeward.

Talking to the 32 skippers who had gone under bare poles either to lay a-hull or to run before the weather, I found that in each case the decision depended very much on the characteristics of the boat, the state of the sea, the physical condition of the crew and often their age too. Six skippers stated that as soon as the wind reached Force 7 and over, they normally dropped all sail and lay a-hull. Some of these were the smaller boats, or those which did not ride well in heavy seas while hove to under sail. Nearly half of the boats surveyed (23) usually went under bare poles once the winds reached gale force (Force 8 and over). These boats were in addition to the previous six who tended to drop sail earlier. All 29 skippers described laying a-hull as their preferred tactic in worsening weather conditions, often going straight for this course of action rather than heaving to under some sort of sail. One skipper remarked that being older and not in a hurry, they preferred to take it easy once the weather got uncomfortable. Whether because of their age or their experience, several of these skippers told me that in their younger days they would have carried on sailing under similar conditions, but have now reached the conclusion that laying a-hull has much to recommend it. On the other hand, two young skippers, both stating that their boats were stiff and handled very well in heavy weather, carried on sailing in gale force winds, but would consider laying a-hull in winds over 50 knots. The skipper of only one boat stated that he carried on sailing regardless of the strength of wind, which he actually had done in winds over Force 10. The boat in question, *Duen* is a heavy displacement double ender meant to take storms in her stride.

Sea anchors or drogues appear to have lost their appeal with most sailors. Even some of the more traditionally minded skippers considered their usefulness as limited and even doubtful. Out of the 50 boats surveyed, 11 carried a sea anchor on board and out of these only four had ever used them. Albert Steele of *Peregrine*, was one of the few skippers using a sea anchor, which he streamed from the stern of his double ended boat. Robbie Millar of *Wrangler* has also streamed a sea anchor from astern when running before heavy weather. At the same time he carried a staysail hauled in tight to steady the boat, letting the wheel free.

Some of the skippers of the boats without sea anchors pointed out that if they desperately need to slow down their boat, they could easily improvise a drag of some sort. With this contingency in mind some boats carried an old car tyre on board, while others had heavy warps available. Bob Miller of *Galatea IV*, who was once caught by a Force 12 storm, trailed a tyre at the end of a 80 ft warp, slowing down the boat from six to four knots without breaking seas over the stern, the boat being easily kept under control all the time.

The principle of slowing down a boat under extreme conditions has been a matter of debate among cruising skippers. Some are of the opinion that one should carry on as fast as possible, attempting to outrun the following seas, while keeping the boat firmly under control and obviously steering by hand. Nevertheless conditions can arise when however fast a boat is moving, she can be overtaken by a following wave. This is what happened to *Sara III* on passage to Panama, when she encountered heavy weather in the Caribbean. A large wave picked up the Swedish 30 foot sloop and projected it forward, causing it to bury its bow and roll over. Fortunately the boat came up with its mast intact but full of water below and in danger of foundering. While she was lying half submerged she was rolled over once more, but again escaped with only minor damage. The skipper Christer Fredriksson told me later that he was convinced that *Sara III* was sailing much too fast for those conditions and that if they had slowed down earlier, probably their misadventure would not have happened.

The survey included a wide range of boats of both heavy and light displacement, large and small, with long and fin keels, so it was very difficult to find a common denominator which would have enabled me to draw some general conclusions on the subject of dealing with heavy weather. However, discussing heavy weather techniques with the most experienced skippers, among whom a dozen had sailed in excess of 50,000 miles, I detected in each of them a profound confidence in the sea-worthiness of their boats. Every one of the skippers I spoke to, who had weathered extreme conditions by dropping all sail, laying a-hull, battening down and leaving the boat to look after itself, stressed the wisdom of such an action and found this tactic more satisfactory than trying to battle with the elements.

Dealing with Emergencies

Several boats included in the survey had their fair share of disasters, in practically every case the crew having to deal with these emergencies themselves, rarely being able to call on outside help. The skippers were asked to describe past emergencies of both mechanical and medical natures, as well as their provisions for dealing with such emergencies in the future.

BREAKAGES AND REPAIRS

Dismasting
Probably the most traumatic failure on a sailing boat is being dismasted, so I tried to find out what provisions boats had for a jury rig if they lost their mast. Several skippers pointed out that they would attempt to salvage as much as possible from whatever rigging and spars were left; 28 boats

Larry Pooter has had his share of emergencies on his trimaran *Spaciety* during two Pacific cruises. On one occasion he repaired a float holed by a whale, while on another was demasted and reached port under jury rig.

carried a good supply of spare wire and cable clips to be used in such an emergency. Two of the older wooden boats carried back-up wooden spars, one of whose skippers remarked that his boat was virtually covered in potential jury rigging.

Two of the boats surveyed had been dismasted, and had reached port under jury rig. The trimaran *Spaciety* managed to carry on with a shorter mast, while *Jellicle* built a bipod mast from a large sculling oar and two spinnaker poles lashed together. The use of spinnaker or running poles as a potential jury rig was mentioned by several skippers some of whom stressed that, especially on sloops, the poles should not be carried attached to the mast, so as not to lose them as well if the boat is dismasted. For the same reason, the mizzen mast on cruising ketches should be rigged entirely independently of the main mast.

Rigging Failure

The most common major emergency experienced at sea was that of broken standing rigging, the breakage being caused either by metal fatigue, failure of the wire terminals or of the turnbuckles. In all eight cases the repairs were carried out at sea, two of them involving several hours work at the masthead. Alan Allmark of *Telemark*, who had to replace a broken turn-buckle at sea, pointed out that the repair could have been much easier if all the turnbuckles on his boat had been the same size, as the only spare he carried was of course not the size that broke.

Another common failure at sea was broken halyards and many skippers stressed the usefulness of having sufficient spare halyards, not only to double up existing halyards, but also to be used in place of a broken stay or shroud. Three skippers described the scary experience of going aloft in a seaway to replace a halyard, two going up on a bosun's chair, the third climbing in relative comfort on his mast steps. One recommendation was the fitting of an extra block and halyard at the masthead prior to a long passage to avoid such a contingency.

Steering Breakdown

The third most common failure was that of steering cables, especially during long runs downwind. Although in all cases the repair was carried out at sea, the skippers who did not have emergency tillers easily available recognised the advantage of such a back-up system. Possibly an auxiliary tiller could be mounted permanently.

Perhaps even more traumatic than losing a mast is losing the rudder. Two boats suffered this misfortune on a long passage, both after extended downwind runs when the rudders had been working continuously, under selfsteering. *Calao* arrived in Barbados after an eighteen day crossing of the Atlantic with the rudder supported by only one bolt after the lower pintles had sheered off. The electric pump barely managed to check the flow of water gushing into the boat through the slack rudder gland and the skipper, Erick Bouteleux, confessed later that there were times when he was convinced that they would never make land. Erick was also distressed by the fact that they saw a flare four days before reaching Barbados, but were unable to turn back in the 25 knot wind, as by now they had to cope not just with the broken rudder but also with a parted forestay; the mast was only held up by the spare jib halyard.

Jocelyn had an equally dramatic arrival in the Marquesas after the rudder was lost altogether during the last few days of the passage from California. The crew managed to keep the boat steering downwind with the aid of an improvised rudder and the selfsteering paddle. With the help of their amateur radio, the crew raised another boat in the Marquesas who came out to rendezvous with them and assisted them safely into Nuku Hiva. *Jellicle* also lost her rudder, but fortunately the transom-hung rudder was secured to the boat with a lanyard, and could be retrieved.

Centreboards

Four boats had various problems with their centreboards, which caused each of their skippers to express doubts about the usefulness of a centreboard on a cruising boat. Three of the boats in question were monohulls, the fourth being the catamaran *Shangri-La* which had their centreboards removed in Punta Arenas, after rounding Cape Horn. False keels were added after removing the centreboards, which in fact improved the catamaran's overall performance.

Engine Problems

Engine repairs were one area in which the self-sufficiency of those experiencing mechanical trouble often let them down and they had to call on outside help, although two skippers managed to carry out spectacular repairs while on passage. Royal McInness of *Mac's Opal* manufactured a new water pump shaft to replace the original, which broke when the cooling water inlet was jammed by pumice stone thrown up by volcanic activity near Tonga. Albert Fletcher of *Duen* (the compulsive tool collector) completely overhauled his engine at sea, even replacing the piston rings. Even if most of the skippers in the survey were unable to carry out repairs of such complexity, all of those experiencing trouble while on passage or in remote anchorages managed to put things right by themselves.

Whales

Collision with whales is a subject that has received considerable publicity in recent years and although three of the yachts included in the survey had collided with whales, the damage sustained was not serious enough to endanger any of the boats in question. Two collisions occurred at night, *Gambol*'s in the South Atlantic, *Galatea IV*'s in the Bismarck Sea, and although both were sailing fast at the time, their strongly built hulls survived the impact without serious structural damage. The trimaran *Spaciety*, while on passage from California to the Marquesas, was surrounded by a large group of killer whales, one of whom rammed one float and holed it. Fortunately the stability of the trimaran was not badly affected and Larry Pooter managed to patch up the 14-in diameter hole with plywood, wood screws and underwater epoxy. The improvised patch lasted for four months and the day after the repair *Spaciety* logged 200 miles.

TOOLS FOR THE JOB

To deal with all these emergencies and many others, a good supply of tools and spares are essential. Among the 50 skippers who were questioned on this point, 26 described the range of tools they carried on board as good, while 14 skippers admitted that their tools were only adequate. Ten skippers considered their tool supply as excellent, which often meant that they were able to help out the less fortunate skippers who had not had the means or foresight to acquire all necessary tools before setting off. It should be pointed out however that what was considered as a good supply of tools by some skippers would appears less than an adequate minimum to others. Some boats did not even have a vice, while others had a complete workshop either in the fo'c'sle or near the engine room. Generally a very good supply of tools was carried on those boats built or fitted out by their skippers. Several boats also had a range of power tools to be used in conjunction with a generator.

The importance of being able to carry out essential repairs was stressed again and again. Dud Dewey who has had his fair share of work on his 50-year old *Hawk* considered the ability to fix everything on one's boat of paramount importance, regarding it as the main ingredient for one's safety. Alan Allmark of *Telemark* also pointed out that above everything else, anyone planning a long distance voyage should attempt to be totally self-sufficient in putting things right on his own boat.

MEDICAL EMERGENCIES

Medical emergencies were fairly infrequent, 39 of the 50 boats having never experienced any accidents or serious medical emergencies. Several people went so far as to specify that they felt much fitter and healthier than when they had lived on land, particularly those liberated from desk-bound jobs.

Of the remaining eleven boats, by far the commonest accidents of a medical nature were broken bones. On seven boats various bones were broken, from legs, noses, elbows and wrists to cracked ribs. One couple were unfortunate enough to both break bones in their feet within days of each other. Fortunately however most of these breakages occurred in port and were dealt with professionally at a local hospital. In mid-ocean, Nancy Lewis of *L'Orion* caught the full force of the winch handle across her face, which smashed her nose and did a lot of damage. Via the amateur radio she spoke to the Honolulu medical centre in Hawaii, the amateur network being able to call on specialist advice 24 hours a day. Within ten minutes of the accident she was talking to a neurosurgeon, who advised her exactly what to do. Although on reaching port Nancy had to fly back to the United States for surgery, she is convinced that the excellent advice she received played a major part in the treatment of her injury, which is now not noticeable.

The second commonest problem experienced was serious infection, of various kinds. All of these were dealt with out of the medical chests carried on board. Burns were quite rare: only one person suffered a serious hot water burn, while another nearly lost an eye after welding without wearing goggles. The only serious illness which involved a return to port was pneumonia contracted after the inhalation of vomit during seasickness. Although not described as an emergency, many people mentioned the high incidence of bacterial infections in the tropics and the constant vigilance necessary to prevent cuts and scratches from turning septic. Many of these infections are caused by the staphylococcus bacteria, which once in the blood stream is very difficult to eradicate and may need antibiotic treatment.

I asked all fifty skippers how they would deal with three hypothetical emergencies, namely broken bones, grave burns and appendicitis. In order to deal with broken limbs, twenty one boats carried a selection of splints, two had inflatable splints; while four boats carried a selection of plaster bandages. Eighteen skippers specified that they could easily improvise splints from existing material on board, such as pencils, rulers and sail battens, whereas five boats had no provision for broken bones at all.

Forty-five boats carried specific ointments and/or special sterile burn dressings in their medical chests to deal with grave burns. One skipper stated that he would prefer to leave a burn untreated until he could reach qualified attention, while another skipper recommended jumping in the sea. This is not quite as crazy as it sounds, for one of the priorities in dealing with a major burn is to cool the skin with cold water and clean sea water will do, if fresh water is not readily available. The two big dangers if a burn is serious are infection, and the loss of fluid leading to shock. One boat did carry an intravenous drip for this contingency. Four boats however had no provision for treating a burn.

Equally, two skippers had no idea how they would cope with appendicitis. Appendicitis is an emergency that worries many potential long distance voyagers, although I have not heard of any cases occurring at sea. Eight crews had solved the problem in advance, by having their appendices removed on purpose prior to their cruise. One couple insisted that they were far too old and had little risk of contracting it, while two skippers said they would race for the nearest port, one of these being able to pack his patient in ice. However the majority of skippers would try and temporarily suppress the appendicitis with large doses of antibiotics until they reached port and these thirty five skippers carried a selection of antibiotics in their medical chests for this purpose. Three skippers were prepared to operate in an emergency. One skipper said that if antibiotics failed to suppress appendicitis in his children he would not hestitate to operate, while another skipper possessed a book, which described the operation step by step. The third skipper was the only one of these with any medical training, being a dentist, and he carried anaesthetic and instruments on his boat for this contingency.

Among those interviewed, four were doctors and four qualified nurses, while the wife of one skipper had undertaken an intensive first aid course before the voyage. Those people who had amateur radio sets on board invariably stated that they would seek qualified advice on medical matters through the amateur radio networks. In the two instances where such an emergency had occurred, expert advice was available within a few minutes of going on the air. Most boats carried a first aid manual and a well stocked medical chest. Nine boats rated the selection carried in their medicine chest as excellent, 29 as good, 11 as adequate and only one skipper admitted that his medical chest was poorly stocked.

Obviously for ocean voyaging the medicine chest should contain a wide variety of medicines.

A basic list for an extended cruise away from immediate medical facilities should include at least the following:

Cotton wool
Various sizes of waterproof adhesive dressings
Sterilised lint

Bandages
Crepe bandages for sprains
Special sterile dressings for burns
Scissors, forceps, safety pins
Thermometer
Disposable syringes and needles
Sterile needles with sutures for stitching
Disinfectant
Antiseptic solution or ointment
Antibiotic powder (eg containing neomycin, powder may be better than
    creams under moist tropical conditions)
Cream or spray for treatment of burns (antibiotics, phenergan)
Antihistamine cream to relieve insect bites and stings
Antihistamine anti-allergic tablets (which can be used for allergies to food,
    insect bites, jelly fish stings etc.)
Antibiotics – ampicillin (covers a wide range of infections, available as a
                syrup for children)
            – tetracycline (not recommended under 12 years, large doses
                can suppress appendicitis in an emergency)
Sulphonamide antibacterial, for urinary tract infections
Laxative
Antidiarrhoeal tablets or kaolin mixture for children
Analgesic – aspirin/paracetamol for minor pain, also for reducing tempera-
                ture
            – pentazocine for more severe pain
Sleeping tablets, useful for helping someone in severe pain to get a good
    night's sleep
Promethazine elixir, such as phenergan, useful as a sedative for a sick child
    and also for allergic conditions, nausea, etc.
Local anaesthetic to allow cleaning and stitching of a major wound
Specific local anaesthetic drops for removing foreign bodies from the eye
Drops and ointments for eye infections (chloramphenicol)
Ear drops for bacterial ear infections
Antifungal preparation for athletes foot and other fungal infections
Antiseasickness tablets
Insect repellant
Sun screen lotion
Antimalarial tablets for prophylactic use (chloroquine)

Medical advice should be sought as to which antibiotics to take, as some
people are sensitive to penicillin and like all powerful drugs, antibiotics

should not be used lightly. Many people carry disposable syringes and needles in case they had to have an injection in countries which do not use disposables, as the risk of hepatitis from improperly sterilised needles and syringes is considerable.

In recent years there has been a resurgence of malaria in many tropical countries and it is highly recommended to start taking the prophylactic drugs before entering a known malarial area. Information on these areas can be obtained from local health authorities, who will also recommend the appropriate drug to take, as some strains of malaria have now become resistant to some of these drugs.

Regulations regarding drugs vary enormously from country to country and some custom officials confiscate certain drugs, such as strong pain-killers like morphine. In several countries however, the laws are very relaxed, and drugs that normally need a prescription, such as antibiotics, can be bought over the counter. Many boats use this opportunity to stock up their medical chest or replace drugs which are past their expiry date.

Dealing mainly with emergencies, I did not include questions on seasickness in the survey, an omission that was pointed out to me by several people, usually those who suffered. Many of these long distance voyagers did suffer from seasickness to a lesser or greater extent, several women being severely afflicted, so that their skippers sailed virtually singlehanded when the weather got rough. From general conversations it appears that most of the sufferers came to terms with this illness in their own personal ways, although recently there have been excellent claims for several new products on the market.

Another problem which caused concern to voyagers in tropical waters was *ciguatera*. This type of fish poisoning is found among fish caught close inshore and near reefs and rarely applies to fish caught by trolling in the open ocean. There is at present no way to detect a toxic fish and toxicity varies from island to island and from species to species. For this reason many crews preferred not to fish at all. Others took the advice of local people, on which fish were edible and which section of a reef to avoid.

Several crews I spoke to had suffered from *ciguatera* intoxications, some of them being left sensitive and unable to eat fish without a recurrence of the symptoms. One of these, a doctor, said he should have known better than to eat moray eel, which is one of the species most likely to be toxic. The symptoms are unpleasant, usually gastrointestinal. There are also particular neurological symptoms such as tingling and numbness. It can be fatal in rare cases and severe attacks can leave the victim weak for months.

Ciguatera has been a mystery illness in the Caribbean and Pacific since it was first described by Columbus, but more about what causes these outbreaks is now becoming known, mainly due to the research team led by Dr Bagnis in Tahiti. He has shown that it is caused by a tiny one-celled plant, which grows on coral and is eaten by fish. These organisms grow quickly on any exposed coral surface and Dr Bagnis has shown how outbreaks of *ciguatera* have followed natural destruction of the coral (such as the outbreak which followed tidal waves and violent storms in the Marquesas in the 1960's) or man-induced destruction, such as blasting, dredging, dumping, construction of quays and breakwaters.

The toxin is cumulative and most likely to affect people who rely on fish to form a major part of their diet, as did several of these voyagers who were on tight budgets. However a large number of areas and fish are trouble free and fresh fish is a tasty dinner sought after by many cruising people, so a few pointers might be helpful. Trolling in the open sea is fairly safe. Of the reef fish, surgeon and parrot fish are most likely to be toxic, also any of the large predators such as snapper, barracuda and grouper. Those over 30 inches may have accumulated toxin and should be avoided. The liver, roe and head should not be eaten and care taken not to puncture the intestines when cleaning. In doubtful areas it is prudent not to eat fish more than once or twice a week and preferably in small portions, as the toxicity is directly related to the amount eaten. Local knowledge is usually reliable.

The Daily Routine

One section of the survey on seamanship concerned itself with the day to day running of the ship at sea. Having dealt with the tactics used in heavy weather, I asked the skippers about their attitudes generally towards reducing sail.

REDUCING SAIL

Seven skippers specified that they reduce sail at night as a matter of principle, regardless of the weather. Another skipper reduced sail occasionally before nightfall, while another only did it when he was singlehanding. On the other hand, when conditions looked doubtful, whether at night or during the day, out of 50 skippers, 41 generally shortened sail, without waiting for the weather to demonstrate its intentions. The remaining nine skippers would carry on under full canvas until the last moment. Some of the skippers of the old school pointed out that nowadays they carry sail much longer than they used to, relying on the superior strength of modern materials.

The majority of boats (30) had slab reefing for their mainsails, 11 had roller reefing, 7 reefed by points, and 2 had both roller and slab systems. Several of the boats which had roller reefing also had points sewn into their mainsail as a measure of precaution in case the roller reefing gear failed. On most ketches the mizzen had points reefing, even when the mainsail itself had slab or roller reefing.

The skippers were also asked to comment on the advantages and disadvantages of their particular reefing system. Those having slab reefing were the most satisfied, mainly because of the speed and ease of operation. The average time estimated by the skippers for putting one reef in their mainsails by this method was three to five minutes.

SAFETY HARNESSES

On six boats, safety harnesses were worn all the time by any person working on deck, not just the skipper. The crews of an additional eleven boats wore harnesses occasionally, both in good and in bad weather. On eight boats harnesses were always worn during heavy weather, while on another eight boats harnesses were worn by those on night watch. The skippers of six boats told me that they wore a harness both at night and in heavy weather. On the remaining eleven boats safety harnesses were virtually never worn, although in most cases they were available on board.

WATCHKEEPING

The system followed for keeping watches varied enormously from boat to boat, from a few who did not keep regular watches at all to a handful of skippers who run their ships along Navy lines. Two factors greatly influenced the watchkeeping; whether the boat was equipped with self-steering or automatic pilot, and the number of crew available. Out of the fifty boats, eight had neither a selfsteering device nor an automatic pilot, five of them being steered by hand continuously and thus being forced to keep a regular system of watches. The crews of the remaining three boats occasionally let the boats look after themselves by trimming the sails and adjusting the tiller. Obviously, the four singlehanders, one of whom had no selfsteering, could not even attempt to keep regular watches, although they tried to keep as good a lookout as possible. This is not always good enough, a fact which is underlined by Jan Swerts' loss of *Tehani III* on a reef in Fiji on a dark night with a heavy sea running. For the previous two days the sky had been overcast and he had been unable to take a sight. The combination of an erroneous DR position and the fact that under these conditions he

Mike Morrish believes that selfsteering gears encourage a lackadaisical approach to watchkeeping, so *Fortuna* sailed around the world without selfsteering and all members of the Morrish family had to take their turn at the helm.

was unable to keep a permanent lookout, had disastrous consequences.

On most boats where watches were kept as a matter of routine, a fixed system of watches only operated at night. In the case of many couples there was a give and take attitude, often the men taking longer watches at night. On most boats with a crew of two, the nights were split into four three hour periods, with two watch and two rest periods. The boats with a crew of three had a similar arrangement, so that in any given night only one crew member had to take two watches. The boats with larger crews generally kept two hour watches, especially those steered by hand. All the older children took watches, although not always by night, while on one boat without selfsteering, the children had to take day and night watches and steer by hand like everyone else. On another boat, two younger children stood their watch together.

The system of watches was generally altered in the event of bad weather, the skippers of shorthanded boats either reducing the length of the watch or putting the entire crew on standby below with only an occasional lookout being kept in the cockpit. A number of boats, especially those with larger crews, did not change their watchkeeping systems in heavy weather.

Even on boats keeping a loose system of watches most of the time, more careful watches were kept when nearing land or sailing close to known shipping lanes. Only two skippers admitted that while on passage away from shipping lanes no watches were kept at all and the entire crew went to sleep at night. On another seven boats, proper watches were also not kept, the skipper relying on crew members and himself to occasionally wake up and look around, the length of these intervals being of various durations, although on most boats this would be done about once every hour. Several boats, whose skippers insisted that nominal watches were kept, should in fact be included in the latter category as their crews' attitude to the chore of keeping watches was very casual in mid-ocean, the watchkeeper often dozing between lookouts.

These conclusions confirmed the findings of my Suva survey, when the system of watches on long distance boats had also been investigated. Among the 62 boats of that survey, on only 45 was a full system of watches in operation, with all adult members of the crew taking their turn at watch-keeping. The remaining 17 boats, and not necessarily those with smaller crews, kept very loose watches, the crew going to sleep at night when on passage and keeping a minimum of watches at other times.

The lackadaisical approach to watchkeeping was condemned by two skippers, who pointed out that they had often seen shipping at night even outside of known shipping lanes, thus invalidating the arguments of those who see no reason why anyone should try and keep awake if there is no shipping around.

'It is only the people who don't keep watches who never see ships at sea, we seem to meet them all the time,' was the comment of Mike Morrish, who decided to sail *Fortuna* around the world without selfsteering gear for the precise reason of having someone on watch all the time.

LIGHTS AT NIGHT

The showing of lights at night is another point of varying opinion and practice. Half of the skippers stated that when on passage and well offshore their boats showed no lights at all. Only four boats showed their correct regulation lights at all times, while two skippers specified that they only had their navigation lights on when in known shipping lanes. However, 15 skippers always showed some kind of light from the masthead, either an all round white, a combined tricolour navigation light, or in the case of four boats, a white flashing strobe light. The remaining four boats burned a paraffin light at deck level, although one skipper who used to do this in the past had abandoned the practice and now preferred to show a masthead light after finding that the bright light at deck level disturbed his night vision.

The boats showing electric lights at night were not necessarily those with more generating power available. I also tried to draw a parallel between showing lights and keeping regular watches, as some skippers had mentioned the fact that they always showed a light if no one was on watch. In fact I found that ten of the boats whose crews kept either casual watches or no watches at all at night, also failed to show any lights. The skippers of the other fifteen boats who did not normally show a light when on passage, did keep watches and specified that the person on watch would put on the navigation lights as soon as a ship was sighted.

MEAL PATTERNS

While talking about the daily routine on these 50 cruising boats, I also asked about the number of meals taken in both normal and bad weather. The crews of 35 boats usually ate three meals a day; on thirteen boats only two meals per day would be served, while on two boats the crew would have only one proper meal plus snacks. On most boats the main cooked meal was served in the evening. Several crews reduced the number of meals in the event of heavy weather, relying mostly on lighter meals and frequent snacks. Thirty of these long distance voyagers however carry on having their usual number of meals regardless of weather conditions.

WEATHER FORECASTS

Taking bad weather in his or her stride is very much a characteristic of the seasoned sailor, so it was not a great surprise to hear that of the 42 skippers who generally listen to weather forecasts, only 28 were influenced by them, usually prior to a departure. Eight skippers stated that they never listen to forecasts, preferring to interpret themselves the information on hand. But even the skippers who are not normally influenced by the forecasts during the relatively safe sailing season, show more prudence if sailing in tropical areas during the hurricane or cyclone season. Many tune in regularly to the WWV and WWVH stations, which give continuously updated information on tropical depressions and storms.

The two stations are operated by the United States National Bureau of Standards, WWV being based in Fort Collins, Colorado, while WWVH is based in Kauai, Hawaii. The services offered by the two stations, both of which broadcast continuously, are varied, their time signals and storm warnings being their most important features. Voice announcements are made once every minute, but to avoid confusion, a male voice is used on WWV and a female voice on WWVH. The WWVH announcement occurs first, at 15 seconds before the minute, followed by the WWV announcement at $7\frac{1}{2}$ seconds before the minute. Every second is marked by a pulse, with the exception of the 29th and 59th second pulses, which are omitted. The specific hour and minute mentioned are in "Coordinated Universal Time" (UTC), which is the same as GMT.

Weather information about major storms or tropical depressions in the Atlantic and Eastern North Pacific are broadcast in voice on WWV at 8, 9 and 10 minutes after each hour. Similar warnings covering the Western Pacific Ocean are given on WWVH at 48, 49 and 50 minutes after each hour. An additional minute (the 11th on WWV and the 51st on WWVH) is sometimes used when there are unusually widespread storm conditions. If there are no warnings in the designated area, this will be indicated in the announcement.

A typical warning would have the following format:

"North Atlantic weather West of 35 West at 1700 UTC: Hurricane Donna, intensifying, 24 North, 60 West, moving northwest, 20 knots, winds 75 knots."

The two stations can also be called up for similar information on the following telephone numbers: WWV on (303) 499-7111 and WWVH on (808) 335-4363.

In several cruising areas there are now amateur radio networks run by landbased enthusiasts, who cater specifically for cruising boats, not only keeping track of their position but also relaying daily weather information. Several skippers mentioned that while on passage they used this information for plotting a more efficient course to take advantage of the existing or impending weather systems. Several skippers, who did not have an amateur license or transmitter, had bought radio receivers which were capable of tuning in to these amateur bands, for the purpose of listening in to weather and other information.

ASTRO-NAVIGATION

While on passage and well offshore, the navigators on 35 boats (who were not always the skipper) relied on two sun sights a day for plotting their position. In 27 of these cases the position was worked out from a morning line of position transferred to a noon sight, whereas the remaining eight navigators generally prefer to transfer the noon latitude to an afternoon sight. On 12 boats the navigators took three sights (morning, noon and afternoon) as a matter of routine, while the navigator of another boat took six sights daily, admitting that as an ex-pilot he took so many sights mainly for pleasure. On five boats the navigators had little use for the noon sight,

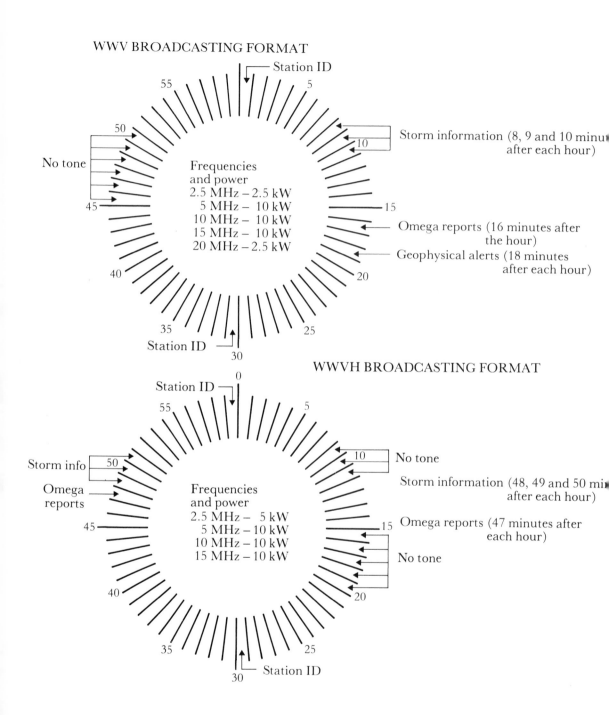

DIAGRAM 1 *The hourly broadcasting schedules of WWV and WWVH*

plotting their position by transferring a morning line of position to an after-noon sight, while on two boats astro-navigation was limited to a daily meridian altitude giving latitude, the longitude being obtained by applying the course and distance run to the noon position. A few skippers pointed out that while in mid-ocean, they took sights only on alternate days, possibly updating their positions from the distance run. Three skippers stated that they found if sufficient to work out their accurate position only once every 48 hours. Nearing landfall, on the other hand, more than half the navigators increased the number of sights taken, often using other celestial bodies as well as the sun. The remaining boats carry on as before, with an average of two sights per day, although their skippers said that they would keep a more alert watch. Gunter Gross of *Hägar*, who has a healthy regard for the many reefs in the South Pacific, told me that when nearing landfall he uses his sextant until it runs hot.

Although relying mostly on the sun for their sights, most navigators occasionally used other celestial bodies in their calculations. For example, 31 navigators had occasionally used the moon, even if some of them extremely rarely, while the remaining 19 had never even attempted to shoot the moon. A similar proportion would occasionally use the stars or planets, with only a few navigators taking star sights routinely.

Canadian singlehander Dick Thuillers of *Because* positively enjoys navigation and takes many sights daily for this reason.

On discussing astro-navigational problems, I found that the sight reduction tables No 249 (AP 3270 in the UK) were the most popular, being used by 73 per cent of the navigators. Less popular were tables No 229 (NP 401 in the UK) used by only 16 per cent of those interviewed. Four skippers used navigator's electronic calculators in working out their sights, while at the other extreme, two skippers swore by the cosine-haversine method.

The cosine-haversine method is just as accurate as the other methods, but is more lengthy in its calculations. It has the advantage of not starting from an arbitrary assumed position, but from the DR position. This is particularly useful when working out a number of simultaneous sights from the same DR position, as in the case of crossed star sights, when the actual plotting on the chart is much easier.

Most navigators choose the Sight Reduction Tables for their simplicity in working out a sight. As a matter of personal preference more navigators in the Suva survey used the Sight Reduction Tables for Air Navigation (HO249) rather than those destined for marine navigation (HO229). The former consists of only three volumes, each covering 30° of latitude, whereas the latter consists of six volumes. The method of calculation for both tables is similar, both being used in conjunction with the Nautical Almanac for the current year.

The main advantage of the navigator's calculators, which have been constantly improved over recent years, is that the basic information contained in the Nautical Almanac is stored in the calculator's memory for many years ahead. As in the case of any calculator, mathematical operations are made much easier, even if some skippers who enjoy astro-navigation think that calculators take the fun out of working out a sight. As the price of these specialised calculators is no longer as astronomical as in their early days, they are becoming increasingly popular. For similar reasons an increasing number of navigators are choosing the simplest method to find out their position, by equipping their boats with satellite navigators. These have certain advantages, particularly when cruising in areas which lack other aids to navigation, such as lights and radiobeacons.

SUGGESTIONS

At the end of each of the 50 interviews that formed the basis of this survey on seamanship, I asked the skippers for their comments or possible suggestions for the benefit of those planning a long voyage. On the question of seamanship in general, several of these experienced sailors stressed that good seamanship begins in port with sound preparation for the intended voyage. Again and again, the skippers emphasised the importance of having a strong and well built boat, that one can trust and have total confidence in. A definite affection for their boats was obvious, especially in the case of those sailors whose vessels had been put to the test by a strong blow or near wrecking, but which had brought them through unscathed.

The paramount importance of a strongly built cruising boat was highlighted by Alain Bloch, who had followed most of Moitessier's recommendations to the letter in building his 38 ft steel ketch *Felix* to a strength well above specification, including watertight bulkheads. Another Frenchman, who did not entirely share this viewpoint, Erick Bouteleux of *Calao*, sarcastically referred to *Felix* as 'the floating strongbox', questioning the wisdom of having a heavy but slow boat, which only takes the fun out of sailing.

Having learned from their own mistakes, several skippers advised other sailors not to rush things. 'Before putting your life's work into a boat, selling your house, giving up your job, try and go first as crew on a longer ocean passage to see what it is all about, before irreversibly committing yourself. And whatever you do, take your wife along,' said George Hartley of *Tara II*. *Incognito*'s skipper, Steve Abney, took this advice one step further when he said, 'Once you have acquired your boat, do not just jump into it and go. Take your time and know your boat well before setting off.'

This view was somewhat refuted by Larry Pooter of *Spaciety*, who was already undertaking his second Pacific voyage. 'Do everything necessary, but don't overprepare for a voyage by spending several years varnishing cans. When you think you are ready, just up and go!'

Discussing specific aspects of seamanship, several skippers, Eric Hiscock among them, pointed out that nowadays people tended to rely too much on engines and engine power. This was a conclusion that could also be drawn from my Suva survey, when the majority of the skippers stressed the importance of having a reliable and powerful energy source at their disposal. According to another veteran sailor, Mike Bales of *Jellicle*, this reliance on auxiliary power sometimes means that boats find themselves in dangerous situations, such as being anchored too near a potential leeshore, motoring too close to a reef under calm conditions, or tied up to a dock with an onshore wind. On *Jellicle* the auxiliary power was provided by an over-sized sweep manned by Mike's Tongan crew Pita Filitonga, while on another engineless boat, *Silverheels*, 300 fathoms of line attached to an anchor were kept in readiness in the forepeak, to be dropped overboard in case the boat was driven near to a reef with no wind to sail her off. The over-reliance on engines has contributed to the loss of several boats, which are discussed in the next chapter.

Yet, in spite of these valid criticisms, the majority of today's sailors would consider cruising without an engine an inconceivable proposition. There is indeed little doubt that engines make cruising more agreeable, often enabling one to get into places, or out of them, which are denied to the engineless boat.

Burghard Pieske, of *Shangri-La*, pointed out that without an engine they would have been in great trouble in Le Maire Strait, in the vicinity of Cape Horn. The combination of opposing tide, strong ocean current and wind produced frightening conditions which the crew described as a witches' cauldron. The sails were slatting so badly in the violent swell that they were threatening to bring down the mast and rigging. Burghard felt that even a strongly built catamaran like *Shangri-La* could have been broken up under such conditions, if they had not had sufficient power to motor out of trouble.

Opinions on seamanship may have changed with time, but most basic rules seem to have remained the same. I found that even the most experienced sailors among those interviewed were not dogmatic and indeed were ready to accept new ideas. Even so, one skipper remarked that there was still a lot to be learned by reading and re-reading the books of old-timers like Slocum and the rest. The unpretentiousness of those oldtimers and their respect for the sea were reflected by many of those interviewed, who described their achievements and experiences with modesty and frankness. The major conclusion to be drawn from talking to such a variety of outstanding sailors is that good seamanship ultimately depends on one's own mental attitude. Mike Bales, who has spent most of his life at sea, best summed this up by saying that above everything else one must learn to be patient.

MIKE BALES AND *JELLICLE* – SIMPLICITY PERFECTED

On the grassy sward behind the quay at Port Vila, the capital of Vanuatu, a dozen New Hebrideans sat in a circle, exercise books in their laps, listening with rapt attention to a thin man with a bushy blonde beard holding forth in fluent Bislama. My first glance around any new port is to see if there is anyone there whom I know, but I could not have been more delighted than meeting this man again. He saw me, interrupted his discourse and greeted me warmly.

'Well, Mike, what are you up to this time?' I asked. He explained that he was giving lessons in seamanship and basic navigation to local fishermen and sailors. In the two months since arriving in Port Vila he had mastered Bislama, the pidgin language, which is widely used in this part of the Pacific.

'I just bought the New Testament in Bislama and read it out aloud a few times. I soon got the feel of the language as most of its words are taken from English.' Mike found that neither the French nor the British administration, who ran the joint colony, had done anything to give formal training to the sailors working on local vessels. Being well qualified for the job as an ex-officer of the Royal Navy, Mike set about filling this demand himself.

Although I had questioned Mike Bales for one of my surveys, when we had met previously in Tuvalu, I was so fascinated by the man and the wisdom he had to impart, that I set my taperecorder rolling and over a bottle of French wine I persuaded him to recount the story of his life.

Sailing without an engine, Mike Bales tries never to find himself in a situation that he cannot sail out of. For this reason his Folkboat *Jellicle* is equipped with a wide inventory of sails.

For the last twenty years Mike has been roaming the oceans in *Jellicle*, a 25 ft Folkboat named after the T. S. Eliot cat that danced in the moonlight. *Jellicle* is simple to the point of being spartan. Mike has no use for an engine, instead preferring a sweep and a full set of sails kept in tip top condition. Below decks, amidst coils of rope, baskets and sacks of basic provisions are two bunks, a navigation table and a simple primus stove. The oldtimers like Joshua Slocum are Mike's mentors and he aims to keep his life as simple as theirs with little time for luxuries. He wouldn't swap *Jellicle* for anything larger or more modern, however much money he had. Mike likes his small Folkboat, which he can sail like a dinghy, but also because it makes him feel closer to the sea he loves and respects.

'Someone once gave me some nice stainless steel cleats, but I took them off after a while and put the old wooden ones back on again. They just spoilt the look of *Jellicle.*' Shiny metal would certainly look out of place on such a basic boat, with no lifelines, a boarded over cockpit to keep out the water and solid wooden spars.

Mike's love for the sea has been with him all his life. His claim to fame that he jokingly boasts about is to be the first officer in the history of the Royal Navy to be courtmartialled twice, found guilty on both occasions, yet still to retire honourably as a Lieutenant Commander on a full pension. The first incident occurred when he was first officer on a submarine and involved in developing a fast turbine engine using a new fuel. His briefcase containing all classified documents relating to the new engine disappeared while Mike was having a few drinks with his fellow officers at a pub near the Admiralty in London. Mike and his commanding officer were found guilty of negligence at a court martial, but were not punished too severely.

From fast submarines, Mike turned his attention to survival in ship's lifeboats, trying to prove that long voyages in such open boats could still be accomplished, as Captain Bligh had so aptly demonstrated. After a few

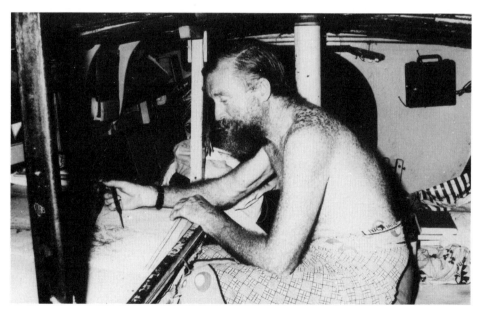

Mike Bales at his navigation table, which occupies much of *Jellicle*'s simple interior.

shorter voyages sponsored by the Navy, Mike selected a crew for a trans-atlantic voyage. Plans were well advanced when at the last moment the top brass cancelled the voyage as being too risky. Mike accepted the decision as any good officer would and so did his crew, except for a young Scotsman, who had also been Mike's crew in his first lifeboat. Utterly dejected and distressed by another ten years in the Navy, the young man threatened to commit suicide. Feeling responsible for the man's plight, Mike wrote to him advising him to desert rather than take his own life. The letter was found and Mike found himself in prison, facing yet another court martial for inciting a rating to desert. Again he was found guilty, although the board was understanding enough to realise that he had acted in good faith and no punishment was exacted.

Mike however had already reached the decision that he had had enough of the Navy and when the opportunity arose two years later, he retired honourably and with a pension. He bought *Jellicle*, not much bigger than a ship's lifeboat, and set off to show that long ocean passages in such a boat were perfectly feasible.

Mike Bales now considers the vast Pacific to be his home, for in *Jellicle* he has covered over 100,000 miles over the years sailing back and forth to every island group south of the Equator. Speaking several Pacific languages, Mike is often to be found in the local library reading books on Pacific history. For several years he made his base in Tonga, running a marine school for young Tongans and commanding a local trading vessel from time to time. Bringing back forgotten skills to a new generation of seafaring islanders gave him both satisfaction and a worthwhile occupation.

For the last few years Mike has always sailed with a Tongan crew, teaching them the art of sailing in a practical way. His first crew, known to everyone as Tonga Bill, is now cruising the Pacific in his own 18-footer, built from secondhand timber and empty crates, in an Auckland dock. Pita Filitonga, another of Mike's disciples, was qualified enough at the age of eighteen to be the navigator on a traditional canoe sailing the thousand miles from Vanuatu to Papua New Guinea for the Pacific Festival of Arts. Having caught the bug from Mike, Pita is building a traditional Tongan canoe, in which he plans to sail around the world.

'I never have girls as crew,' laughs Mike, 'I find them too distracting,' and he launched into a story about how he nearly lost an expensive charter schooner in the Caribbean, when both he and his first mate were head over heels about the same girl in the crew. Too much in love to think straight, he once let the boat get too near a reef, was unable to go about, and ran aground. It never occurred to him to start the engine; he just watched it all happen in slow motion. Ironically, the Royal Navy frigate which came to the rescue was commanded by an ex-colleague, who laughingly told Mike, 'Fortunately, no court martial for you this time, Commander Bales.'

After that episode, Mike has banned women from his ship, except as visitors in port.

'No woman would live this frugally anyway,' Mike added with a smile, as he watched my wife Gwenda casting an eye over *Jellicle*'s uninviting interior. While living modestly and frugally, Mike still enjoys life and lives it to the full. He has a great ability to get on with people and is an extremely patient teacher, a quality much appreciated by the islanders. Anyone can learn a lot from him, especially about the virtues of patience and simplicity for those whose lives are involved with the sea.

The morning I left Port Vila, I met Mike walking along the main street with a big coil of rope slung over his shoulder.

'Where are you off to now?' I asked.

'Believe it or not to the prison. I have permission to give lessons on seamanship to the inmates.'

'And what is the rope for?'

'Oh, today's practical lesson is on knots and splices.'

'You had better watch they don't learn about rope ladders, as it won't be the Royal Navy judging you this time,' I teased him. His freckled face lit up in a wide grin.

'All right. No rope ladders, I promise.' Unfortunately, there are not many people like Mike Bales left in this fast moving world of ours.

*   *   *

Shortly after speaking to Mike in Port Vila, I met the Bulgarian couple Julie and Doncho Papazov, who had successfully crossed both the Atlantic and the Pacific oceans in a ship's lifeboat. When the Papazovs made their landfall from Gibraltar on the coast of Cuba, they were immediately arrested as spies. No one would believe that they had sailed all that distance in such a small boat, and when, on their insistence, the Cubans phoned the Bulgarian embassy in Havana the reaction was the same.

'What two Bulgarians in a sailing boat? Impossible. Of course they are spies, comrade, so just keep them locked up.' Eventually phone calls back home got their voyage confirmed and they were let out of jail, but they still

Julie and Doncho Papazov learned about long distance sailing on converted lifeboats. Later with daughter Yana on their 45 ft ketch *Tivia*, they became the first Bulgarians to sail around the world.

regret their decision to make for Cuba in the naive hope that a fellow Communist country would give them a friendlier reception. Later on I met the Papazovs in Bulgaria, where they had just completed a circumnavigation on their 45 ft ketch *Tivia*.

ASLAN'S EXPERIMENT

Few people can have left home on a cruise as green and inexperienced as Beverly and Scott Wilmoth. The idea to go cruising was just an impulse. One summer Sunday some friends had taken them for a sail on Lake Ray Hubbard in Texas. Later over drinks they all agreed that sailing around the world would be fun. It certainly sounded more fun than the life Beverly and Scott were leading as garage owners in Texas. Without giving it much more thought, they decided to embark on a world cruise. 'I've always been impulsive,' smiled Beverly.

A few months later they bought a 27 ft sailing boat, to learn a bit about sailing, although it took them several months to realise that they had rigged it the wrong way. Texas was definitely not sailing country, so they set off for California to look for another boat. They were so taken by the second boat they saw, *Aslan*, a 41 ft Kettenburg fibreglass sloop, that they immediately bought her. From then on, events began to snowball and only one year after their first Sunday afternoon sail, they had already set a date for departure. In the turmoil of leasing Scott's business, selling their house and other preparations, they had had little time to learn about boat-handling, seamanship or such practical matters as navigation. They left San Diego in 1977 for the two thousand mile trip to Hawaii as almost complete innocents.

The only chart for the area which they had on board showed Hawaii as a speck in the corner. In the rush before leaving, Scott had found a young Australian yachtsman in San Diego harbour, who showed him how to use the sextant and work out a sight. After six days on the ocean, Scott decided to have a go at his first sight. At noon he managed to get a reading, but when the pair tried to work out their position, they found they had forgotten completely even which books and tables the Australian had told

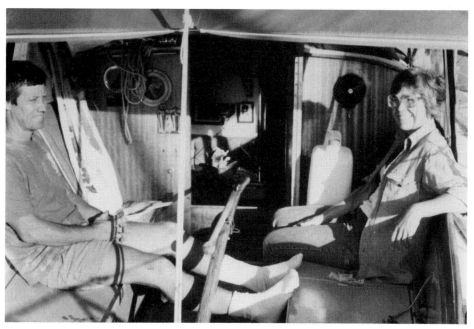

Aslan's crew relaxing in port after a hard sail.

them to use. For four days they pored over Mary Blewitt's manual of navigation, figuring out how to do the calculations. No wonder then that nineteen days after leaving San Diego, when Hawaii appeared just where it should be, it gave them one of the biggest thrills of their landlubbing lives.

After three months in Hawaii, they sailed on to the Marquesas and across the Pacific to Tahiti, Samoa, Tonga and Fiji, gradually becoming more confident in their navigating skills, with each departure being less chaotic than the one before. It was only when *Aslan* sailed across the date-line on the way to Fiji, that they realised something was amiss. First Beverly, then Scott tried to work out their sights, but it did not make sense at all. No one had warned them that west of the 180° meridian, degrees of longitude are counted from west to east, and that sights have to be worked out in a different manner. So it was back to the navigation manual to find the answer. They were lucky to make Fiji, for strong unpredictable currents, unlit reefs and navigational mistakes around the 180° line result in several boats coming to grief in Fijian waters every year.

In their innocence or luck, they had chosen in *Aslan* a well made solid boat with graceful lines, well equipped and able to take them safely across the oceans. Aware of their shortcomings and not being ashamed of their lack of experience, they were always eager and willing to learn from others who were more experienced. After spending six months in New Zealand improving and maintaining *Aslan*, they left for Australia across the notorious Tasman Sea.

'We have never left a port so well prepared,' Beverly told me on the eve of their departure. Although the idea of a world cruise had been in the back of their minds, they had set off for only one year to see if they enjoyed sailing. They found that they loved it.

'We met great people and just sailed farther and farther. By the time we got to New Zealand, it was just as easy to go on around.' After nearly three years of cruising, they sailed via South Africa across the Atlantic to the Gulf of Mexico and Texas, having logged over 30,000 miles on *Aslan*. They were no longer green, but experienced sailors. Aptly, their personal motto is simply

'Learn as you go!'

CHAPTER FOUR

Why Lost? Thirty losses investigated

The Fastnet disaster of 1979 sent shivers down the spine of every sailor throughout the world. 'Could it happen to me?' was probably the first thought that flashed through everyone's mind, especially in the case of those of us who were actually on the ocean, cruising in faraway places, away from the magnificent rescue facilities that the participants in the Fastnet Race had been able to call upon. We were in the South Pacific at the time, on passage from Tuvalu to Fiji. The stark announcement on the BBC World Service news about the heavy loss of life on the opposite side of the globe prompted me to make an immediate check of all safety features on board *Aventura*.

For the last two years we had been sailing in some of the least frequented areas of the world and I had always been aware that if disaster struck, we had absolutely no chance of calling on outside help and had to solve any crisis alone. We had no radio transmitter on board and were thus totally self-reliant. If the worst came to the worst and we *had* to abandon ship, we had at our disposal both an inflatable liferaft and a hard dinghy, which was lashed on the foredeck from where it could be launched quickly if necessary. The raft container was kept near to the cockpit, so as to be able to be launched in the shortest time possible. Also close to hand was a waterproof plastic box containing emergency rations, first aid kit, fishing gear and all the essential items one would need for survival after emergency abandonment. While taking every possible precaution in case we were forced to abandon ship, my main concern had always been to make the boat herself as seaworthy as possible. As more details emerged about the Fastnet disaster, it became increasingly obvious that if some of those involved had had more confidence in their boats, and ultimately in them- selves, many more would have survived.

Unfortunately, sailing boats are lost regularly and not only in such tough ocean races, even if it takes a disaster of this magnitude to attract the attention of a media, often only interested in disaster stories. The Fastnet tragedy prompted me to think about boats that had been lost recently and I was shocked to find that I could list immediately twenty such boats that I knew about personally. Out of the one hundred or so boats included in my surveys, at least three have since been lost, while another eight have narrowly missed the same fate.

Over the last ten years the number of long distance voyages has increased dramatically and probably the increase in boats lost is proportional to this. Yet, compared to earlier small boat voyages, we have at our disposal today better charts, fairly reliable weather information, satellite tracking and warning of tropical depressions and storms, advanced aids to navigation, and improved instruments. Furthermore, present day boats are generally made of stronger materials than those of our predecessors. Taking all these factors into consideration and even allowing for the fact that some of today's voyages are perhaps more ambitious than those of yesteryear, these losses still appear to be disproportionally high.

While sailing from the Pacific back to the Mediterranean, I have gathered material on thirty boats lost under a variety of conditions and circumstances, and later tried to analyse the reasons why they were lost. The major causes for the loss of the boats in question appear to be collision, sinking or foundering in open water for various reasons, and wrecking on reefs or shores. In several cases the causes were interrelated.

Collision with Flotsam

Collision caused the sinking of four of these boats. Two New Zealand boats sailing in the Pacific, *Pono* and *Southern Kiwi*, hit unidentified objects at night and sank quickly. Both crews abandoned ship and were later rescued. Unfortunately, at night it is virtually impossible to avoid such objects, which may include containers lost by ships (those containing a lot of polystyrene packing do not sink and could theoretically float forever), fragments of docks or jetties, navigation buoys adrift, or tree trunks.

Whales

Another two boats, also from New Zealand, *Snow White* and *Dauntless*, both collided with whales and were lost equally quickly. Both collisions occurred in broad daylight. *Snow White*, returning home from a race in Fiji, was bowling along at over seven knots and, although hand-steered and with a full watch on deck, only saw the injured whale *after* the collision. *Dauntless* was at the time on passage from New Caledonia to New Zealand, motoring in calm weather. Three sperm whales, a male, female and calf, were sighted at a safe distance, but the calf made for the boat for a closer look. Probably sensing danger, its mother rammed the boat, holing it amidships. With blood spouting from the injured whale, the bull also joined in the attack, the violent impact lifting the light displacement 50 ft boat out of the water. The crew managed to launch the two liferafts, while skipper Frank Innes-Jones sent out repeated Mayday calls on his portable ham radio, which had been wired up to an emergency battery kept for just such an event. The signal was picked up by an amateur enthusiast in New Zealand, which triggered off a search operation, and the shipwrecked sailors were rescued by a freighter less than 24 hours after losing their boat.

Ironically, we had parted company with *Dauntless* only a few days earlier in Port Vila, when I had been involved in a lengthy but friendly argument with Frank on the merits of using light displacement boats for cruising. I had expressed my worries about the inherent weakness of a lightly built hull, only to be reassured by Frank that *Dauntless* had been equipped with watertight bulkheads fore and aft for this very reason. Unfortunately, not even an experienced skipper like Frank could have foreseen the million-in-one chance of being rammed amidships by an infuriated sperm whale.

This was, incidentally, Frank and Shirley Innes-Jones second shipwreck. Thirty years earlier, while returning home on the coastal trader *Awahou*, she hit a reef south of Fiji, but was fortunately kept afloat by her cargo of empty oil drums. Five days later they were all saved by an American cruiser.

Although there is still little documented evidence that whales will attack entirely without provocation, collision with a whale either resting or sleeping on the surface may well result in an attack either by the wounded animal itself or by one of its mates.

The trimaran *Spaciety* while on passage to the Marquesas was surrounded by a pod of killer whales, one of whom rammed one float and holed it, although the skipper Larry Pooter was not sure if it was meant as an aggressive action or was just curiosity. He felt that the whales were not purposively aggressive, as they appeared concerned and stayed with the boat, peering in through the hole at him as he repaired the hull, an action he found quite disconcerting.

Two boats, *Galatea IV* and *Gambol*, collided with whales at night, the former in the Bismarck Sea off New Guinea, the latter in the South Atlantic. Both were sailing at six to seven knots at the time and were fortunate to escape without structural damage. *Galatea IV* arrived in Madang after the collision with all stanchions and the pushpit stove in along one side by the whale's gigantic tail, which passed only a few inches over the head of Marg Miller, who was sitting on watch in the cockpit, too

Strongly built *Galatea IV* survived a collision at night with a whale in the Bismarck Sea.

shocked to move. While on passage from South Africa to Brazil, *Gambol* encountered one day a large number of whales, but they all kept away from the boat. During the night however, while running fast before the South Easterly tradewinds, the boat collided with a whale and came to an abrupt halt. A slight leak developed forward, where the fibreglass sheathing had cracked, but subsequent inspection of the hull revealed only slight damage to the sturdily built boat. Like *Galatea*'s skipper, Stuart Clay was also thankful that *Gambol* was strong enough to withstand such an impact.

Collisions with Ships

Being run down or colliding with a ship did not appear to be the cause of any loss among my sample of thirty boats, although it could be one of the explanations for at least two boats, which have mysteriously disappeared in the Pacific for unknown reasons. From Slocum to Colas, sailing boats have disappeared at sea without trace, and being run down by a ship is still regarded by many as possibly the greatest danger at sea. The only solution to this is careful watchkeeping.

Weather

Several boats have been lost recently during tropical revolving storms, which are called cyclones, hurricanes or typhoons depending on the area in which they occur. The skippers of these boats took the risk of sailing through a known hurricane area during the hurricane season. The yacht *Drambuoy* left Mauritius bound for South Africa too late in the season, which in the South Indian Ocean extends from November until March and was caught on Christmas Eve by Cyclone Claudette. *Drambuoy* disappeared without trace. A similar fate befell *Crusader* whose skipper also disregarded all warnings and set off across the Bay of Bengal in the midst of the cyclone season and hasn't been heard of since. The fast racing trimaran *Captain Bligh* was lost during the cyclone season in the South Pacific. The skipper had assured me earlier, when I spoke to him in the Solomon Islands about his intended route across the cyclone area, that his boat was so fast he could outrun any tropical depression.

DIAGRAM 2. *World Distribution of Tropical Storms.*

Area	Jan	Feb	Mar	Apr	May	Jun	Jul	Aug	Sep	Oct	Nov	Dec
Caribbean and Southern USA					■	■	■	■	■	■	■	
East North Pacific						■	■	■	■	■		
West North Pacific						■	■	■	■	■	■	■
North Indian Ocean					■	■	■	■	■	■	■	■
South Indian Ocean	■	■	■									■
South West Pacific	■	■	■								■	■

LIGHTNING

Being struck by lightning could be another cause of mysterious disappearances, at least one tropical thunderstorm I have been through was of such incredible violence, that it left no doubt in my mind whatsoever that any of those tremendous bolts of lightning would probably spell the end of us if we were struck. This was between Samoa and Tonga. Another area of violent thunderstorms, especially during the North West monsoon, is the Bismarck Sea. *Rigadoon* was struck by lightning during such a storm off northern New Guinea and, although most of their equipment was earthed, all electrical gear on board was destroyed. Even their cassettes were erased. Fortunately the structure of the boat suffered no damage.

Fittings Failure and Structural Damage

While one can keep out of the hurricane belt during the bad season, some internal faults are more difficult to detect. Although none of the cases in point were known to be lost as a result of internal faults, apart from engine failure which is considered later on, two boats narrowly escaped being lost. A child sleeping under the table raised the alarm on board the South African yacht *Seafari*, which was taking part in the Cape to Rio race, when seawater started gushing into the main cabin from a mysterious source. The crew were on the point of abandoning the boat when the skipper fortunately traced the leak to a loose hose clip on the engine seawater intake.

When the French yawl *Calao*, while on passage from Wallis to Fiji in heavy weather, dropped off a wave, the force of the fall split open a seam on the twenty year old wooden boat. Although taking water heavily, by using all pumps and moving the engine intake hose to draw water from the bilge, *Calao* reached the island of Futuna. With the help of friends from the yacht *Alkinoos*, the crew temporarily patched up the leak.

Other possible internal causes, which could have fatal results, are the destruction of through-hull fittings by electrolysis, and explosion caused by bottled gas or other volatile materials. Corroded seacocks account for the sinking of several boats at their moorings, although I know of no yacht lost as a result of such a failure while actually cruising. Nevertheless the danger of a skin fitting or a seacock passing away while at sea is very real, and on *Aventura* I have prepared a selection of wooden plugs which fit every hole in the hull. Each plug has its destination clearly written on its side, and they are kept at an arm's length from the cockpit. In an emergency a plug could be quickly hammered into the failed fitting from the outside. In an equally accessible place a snorkel and a mask are kept ready to grab in an emergency.

An explosion on board can also spell disaster, and such a violent explosion has been suggested as the reason for the disappearance of *Valhalla*, while on passage from American Samoa to Tonga. Some wreckage of the boat, which had a radio transmitter on board, but didn't send out a call for help, was later found washed ashore in Western Samoa.

Wrecking

By far the majority of the boats whose loss I have investigated were wrecked on reefs or shores, or were driven ashore while at anchor in bad weather. The losses can be attributed to a multitude of causes, such as erroneous navigation, poor watchkeeping, over-reliance on the engine, bad planning, running for shelter, anchoring in exposed places or failure of ground tackle.

NAVIGATIONAL ERROR

At least eight of the 30 boats concerned were lost as a direct result of errors of navigation, although these were often compounded by some of the other factors already mentioned.

Six boats were wrecked at night and, because the skippers thought that they were in a safe place, no one was on watch when disaster struck. Several of the skippers admitted afterwards that if someone had been on deck, the reef could have been either sighted or heard in time, and possibly avoided. As three of these were singlehanded (*Tehani III*, *Moana* and *Happy*), a permanent watch was out of the question, although in all three cases the reefs which they struck were several miles off their estimated positions. *Tehani* was lost on a reef in Fiji's Lau Group only minutes after her skipper, Jan Swerts, had gone to his bunk convinced that he was well past a particular reef. Ray Quint lost his *Moana* under similar circumstances in Micronesia, while the singlehanded skipper of *Happy*, on passage from Malaysia to Sri Lanka, missed the latter altogether and ended up on a reef in the Maldive Islands, nearly 400 miles further west.

The only conclusion I can draw from some of these wreckings is that a haphazard approach to watchkeeping has been brought about by many skippers relying completely on selfsteering. As far as I know all nine boats wrecked on reefs were on selfsteering when lost. Similarly, it appears that people rely greatly on their engines to get them out of trouble. The loss of *Grockle*, at Penrhyn in the Northern Cook Islands, most probably could have been avoided if a flat battery had not failed to start her engine, when the boat was being driven onto the nearby reef by swell and current. *Tio Pepe*, after having been sailed successfully by a delivery crew from England halfway around the world to Fiji, was wrecked one hundred miles from her destination for exactly the same reason, an engine which failed to start promptly. The loss of a French boat on the windward reef at Wallis, also in the South Pacific, was equally traumatic as the boat had been totally becalmed for several hours and the hapless crew could only watch helplessly as the boat was eventually driven onto the reef by the swell and destroyed. Again, it was a non-starting engine that got the blame.

Unfortunately it is generally impossible to anchor on the ocean side of a coral barrier reef as the coral rises almost vertically from the ocean bottom. Depending on the size of the boat and the availability of a sufficiently powerful and reliable outboard engine, some people have managed to tow themselves out of danger with their dinghy, while on engineless *Jellicle*, a large sweep has been used to get the 25 foot Folkboat out of a dangerous area when there was no wind.

Over-reliance on other equipment apart from engines can also have disastrous results. Relying on his dead reckoning, the skipper of a French boat on an overnight passage from Tahiti to Bora Bora, did not even bother to go on deck, when the crew on watch woke him up as it was getting light. Instead, he switched on the radar and waited for it to warm up. Seconds later, the boat struck the reef on the southern extremity of Bora Bora, which should have been a mile away according to his dead reckoning. Having satellite navigation equipment on board did not prevent another boat from ending up on a reef north of Indonesia, but at least it enabled the skipper to positively identify the reef under his keel and radio his exact position via an amateur radio network. An American naval ship was sent to his rescue from the Philippines, and the boat was eventually towed off and saved.

In two of the areas where some of these boats were lost, Fiji and the Red Sea, strong unpredictable currents make navigation extremely difficult at all times, even more so when no sights can be taken because of overcast skies. Several skippers of the boats lost in these areas complained to me about the frustration of not being able to take a sight for several days and being forced to estimate their position without sufficient reliable information at hand. I could well sympathise with them, as on one occasion, while on passage from Tonga to Fiji, I was unable to take any sights at all for three days and crossed this reef infested area relying solely on my eyes and ears.

AT ANCHOR

Striking a reef at night in a dangerous area, which may be difficult or even impossible to avoid passing through, could be described as bad luck. Losing one's boat while at anchor is, on the other hand, an entirely different matter. Two boats, one at Easter Island, the other at Pitcairn, were driven ashore and destroyed while their crews were visiting the islands. The anchorages at both these islands are known to be unreliable, yet the boats were left unattended for long periods during squally weather. The mast of the wrecked Japanese boat now serves as a flagpole at Hangaroa village on Easter Island, a grim reminder to any sailor venturing that far off the beaten track, never to lose sight of his boat, while visiting the mysterious stone giants. A ferrocement boat from California was the victim of bad weather on Pitcairn, and the inhabitants of this remote island still recall bitterly how they stood by helplessly as the boat pounded on the rocks in the same spot where their mutinous ancestors had burnt and scuttled their *Bounty*. They were upset because they had repeatedly warned the skipper to return to his boat in the deteriorating weather. A third boat was lost at Niue, another island in the South Pacific, while her crew were visiting ashore. The boat had been left on a mooring laid down for visiting boats, but during an unexpected onshore squall the mooring cable parted and the boat was blown onto the rocks.

Aventura at anchor in Bounty Bay, the exposed anchorage on Pitcairn island, where one always has to be ready to put to sea at short notice if the weather changes.

Anchoring in exposed places is a risk that is sometimes difficult to avoid if one wishes to visit the less frequented places. The Australian boat *Korong II* was nearly lost in such an anchorage in the Ha'apai group of Tonga, when it was driven onto the nearby reef by a strong squall during the night. The boat had been anchored so close inshore, that before the engine could even be started, she hit the reef, damaging the propeller blades and jamming the rudder. Unable to steer or move, the boat was driven onto the reef from where it was towed off later the next day by a local coaster. Fortunately, being a well built boat, the fibreglass hull survived twelve hours of pounding and came off with no structural damage. In the Pacific, squalls like the one which *Korong II* experienced can sometimes occur *contrary to the prevailing winds*, even during the hurricane-free trade wind season. This should certainly be borne in mind when choosing an anchorage.

The loss of an additional three boats should also be included in this category, as they were lost while at anchor, their skippers having chosen to remain and cruise in the hurricane belt during the wrong season. *Ocean Rover* and *Chimera* were completely broken up as the eye of cyclone Meli swept over their anchorage off Kandavu, in Southern Fiji. According to *Chimera*'s crew the unshackled fury of the cyclone was so violent that amidst the turmoil they did not even realise that their boat had been dismasted. In the calm eye of the storm they managed to swim ashore, together with *Ocean Rover*'s skipper. Two crew members of *Ocean Rover* were drowned and when the storm had passed over, nothing was left of the two boats except some floating debris. The trimaran *Zoom* was driven ashore and broke up in Honiara in the Solomon Islands, by a vicious onshore squall, known to occur regularly at that time of year.

Running for shelter in bad or worsening weather has often been regarded as more dangerous than remaining at sea, and the loss of *Maruffa*, described in detail on the following pages, is a case in point.

With more or less justification, most of the skippers who have lost their boats attribute at least part of the loss to sheer bad luck, but none more than the Japanese singlehander Yukio Hasebe of *Pink Mola Mola*. While sailing along the coast of Queensland, in Australia, he fell overboard, although he continued to be attached to the boat by his safety harness. However hard he tried to climb back on board, he could not manage to do it as the boat continued to sail very fast steered by her vane, towing behind her the unfortunate skipper. Yukio could do nothing but watch helplessly as the boat eventually steered herself onto the rocks.

Like Yukio Hasebe, many of the crews, although losing their boats, had the fortune to be rescued, even if this included some harrowing experiences,

Another casualty among the singlehanders, Yukio Hasebe lost his *Pink Mola Mola* off the coast of Queensland.

like being stranded for several days on a reef or drifting helplessly in a life-raft. Nevertheless, several lives were lost among the thirty boats that made up this sample, including the complete crews of four boats, three of which left no trace or wreckage.

Reducing the Risks

The main reason for examining carefully the various causes for the loss of a number of boats in the foregoing pages was not so much curiosity, but primarily the wish to single out those dangers which could be avoided. The majority of the thirty losses that came under my scrutiny might have been avoided, and this should be a great encouragement to all those who put to sea in small boats. What then can one do to increase one's safety?

Collisions at night with unlit objects, often low in the water, are practically impossible to avoid, unless one is prepared to stop altogether and heave to, an unacceptable proposition for any cruising boat. Nevertheless, risks can be minimised by reducing speed at night in areas known to be littered with floating debris or frequented by whales. Without doubt a strongly built hull can greatly reduce the risk of sinking if such a collision cannot be avoided, as in the case of *Galatea IV* and *Gambol*, both of whom collided with whales at night while sailing at full speed. Shortly after hearing of *Galatea*'s encounter with a whale in the Bismarck Sea, we sailed through the same area on *Aventura*. Throughout the day we kept a good lookout for whales or floating trees, while every night at sunset I shortened sail to reduce speed to about four knots, a speed at which I feel a well built boat should be able to survive such a collision without sustaining major damage. Several times during those nights we heard a dull thud as we bumped into tree trunks and other debris washed out to sea by the heavy monsoon rains. One year later, while on passage from Malaysia to Sri Lanka, my daughter Doina asked one evening why we didn't slow down at night any more.

Aventura's strong fibreglass hull built by the Tyler company to a Van der Stadt design, took a heavy impact with a log without sustaining structural damage.

'No need to do it here,' I replied confidently, 'as there are neither floating trees nor whales in this part of the Indian Ocean.'

That very night at 01.00, during Gwenda's watch, I was thrown out of my bunk as the boat hit something hard. We were doing six knots at the time, running under poled out twin jibs, yet the collision was so violent that *Aventura* came to a complete standstill. I ran on deck with a light and saw a massive tree trunk slowly roll up from under our keel. The menacing black shape, with stumps sticking out where thick branches had broken off, disappeared behind our stern as *Aventura* slowly picked up speed in the twenty knot wind. To my great relief the bilge appeared to be dry when I checked it, but a later underwater inspection in port revealed more damage to the hull than I had expected, the hull having been badly scored by the trunk along the entire forefoot. I have no doubt that we were only saved by the strength of our hull and I am equally convinced that some boats I know would probably have been sunk by such a collision.

The very next day in broad daylight, sailing along at full speed in some of the most glorious weather we have ever encountered, we saw a large whale right in front of us sleeping on the surface. Its gigantic back was showing only inches above the water and, as we hastily altered course to avoid it by a few feet, it opened one eye and cast us a nasty glance, probably cursing us for having disturbed its siesta.

'No tree trunks or whales around here Dad?' asked Doina with a cheeky smile on her face. It was a lesson I am never likely to forget.

Keeping a good lookout at all times can undoubtedly play a major part in reducing one's risk. Even if a navigational mistake has been made or if overcast weather prevents the taking of accurate sights, a good pair of eyes can still avoid disaster. Sailing at night on dead reckoning along the coast of Papua New Guinea, the New Zealand boat *Maamari* just had time to go about and avoid a reef, which was heard and later seen by the crew on watch. The navigator had laid a course fairly close to the reef, relying on seeing a light before altering course. In fact the light had been out of action for some time, and this example shows how good watchkeeping can avoid disaster.

Even the best and most up-to-date instruments do not make a lookout obsolete, and the fact that modern ships equipped with the entire range of navigational instruments are still wrecked proves this point. Generally, reefs do not show up well on small radar screens, yet I found that reefs on the windward side of islands always break, except in the calmest of weathers, and are thus audible and visible even at night. Even on the lee side, reefs are often visible, especially when there is some swell. Of the nine boats in this sample, which were lost on reefs, four were wrecked during the day and it is a matter of speculation if the remaining five could have taken avoiding action in time. Two of these skippers, both singlehanders, admitted that the reefs could have been either heard or seen, had they been awake at the time.

A strongly built hull like the steel *Karak* can greatly reduce the risk in the event of a collision.

KARAK

In extremely bad weather, however, the sighting of reefs can be almost impossible. Unable to make the entry into the lagoon at Wallis before dark, I remember one unpleasant night hove-to above 25 miles off the reef. Torrential rain and flying spray in the forty knot wind made me realise it would be impossible to distinguish a reef until almost on top of it. Under such conditions one must be exaggeratedly prudent.

The avoidance of collision in good light should be possible by all those prepared to keep a permanent lookout, so that avoiding action can be taken before it is too late. The days when power gave way to sail without question are fast disappearing and, with an ever increasing number of ships being reluctant to alter course to avoid a small sailing boat in their path, it is safer to assume that a ship on a converging course is not going to give way and to take whatever action is necessary in good time.

On several occasions, both in broad daylight and at night, we have been forced to take avoiding action as the ships in question did not appear to be aware of our presence and most certainly showed no intention of altering course. This is something that has also happened to many of the skippers I spoke to. Once, having to use my engine to get out of the way of a small freighter in bad weather in the Black Sea, a wave lifted *Aventura* up level with its bridge. From 100 feet away I looked straight through the bridge. It was completely deserted with no one at all on watch.

There is no real excuse for neglecting one's watches *even when off known shipping lanes*, as the most deserted areas of the ocean can be crossed by fishing boats, naval ships, research vessels, submarines and, of course, other yachts. In one particular incident, two cruising yachts did collide at night off Tonga, fortunately gently and without much damage. Both skippers were convinced that the area was so deserted that it wasn't necessary to have anyone on watch, nor were they showing any lights. When the skippers had got over the shock of this mild collision, they at least had the pleasure of realising that they were friends and hadn't bumped into each other since leaving California.

Careful and accurate navigation should be the prerequisite for any cruising boat, yet almost one third of the boats in question were wrecked as a direct result of gross navigational errors. During my previous surveys I had the chance to discuss the subject of navigation with over one hundred skippers and I was surprised in several cases at the lackadaisical approach to navigation in general, especially to astro-navigation. Many skippers appeared to rely too heavily on dead reckoning and failed to update their positions regularly, with the result that if and when the weather did close in, their positions were inaccurate and badly out of date. Besides keeping a carefully updated position, many of these boats would not have got into trouble if their skippers had decided to heave to, either to wait for daylight, for better weather or, at least, for a clear sky to take a reliable sight.

Many skippers however, like myself, prefer to take as many sextant sights as possible, allowing a continual update of position. After having lost half a dozen towed log impellers to hungry fish, who nonetheless ignore the tastefully decorated lures trailing behind *Aventura*, I have stopped using the log in areas where the rate and direction of the currents are known to be unreliable. My guestimates, based on the latest sights, have become increasingly accurate, although I still prefer to stop and heave to the moment I start having doubts about our actual position. As darkness usually lasts twelve hours in the tropics, we have sometimes hove to as far as thirty miles from our intended objective. Such a wide safety margin would have taken care of any current up to $2\frac{1}{2}$ knots and still allowed us to reach our destination by noon the following day, if we started sailing again as soon as it got light.

The Lau or Eastern Group of Fiji is one of the most dangerous areas in the world; several cruising boats come to grief in these reef strewn waters every year. Although the charts are fairly accurate, only a few dangers are marked by lights and the distances are too great to allow the prudent navigator to pass all dangers in daylight. Currents in the area are strong and unpredictable. To make things even more difficult than they already are, most boats arrive in this reef area after a 200 mile passage from Tonga. Although well to the east of the 180° meridian, Tonga has decided to keep the same date as her nearest neighbour to the west, Fiji. As a result, local time in Tonga is GMT +13; rather than GMT −11, as it should be. This also means that the official day in Tonga is one day ahead of her GMT day. Most boats arrive in Tonga from the east, unaware that in fact in Tonga today means tomorrow. After their first visit ashore, all crews change their time and date to the local standard and often do not give the matter another thought. The real problem starts on the next leg of the voyage, to Fiji, when many navigators forget to set back their time by 24 hours. Working out a sight by using the wrong day entry in the Nautical Almanac can result in latitude errors of up to twelve miles, with possible fatal consequences in an area where some passes are only a few miles wide.

Poor watchkeeping, over-reliance on selfsteering devices, and gross errors in navigation are interrelated factors which have together caused the loss of at least ten of the boats examined. Obviously, the problem was compounded by the fact that several of these were singlehanded. Yet even singlehanders can try and keep out of trouble by following the example of old salt Albert Steele of *Peregrine*, who often prefers to heave to and rest in daylight, thus giving other ships a chance to see him. It also allows him to be alert at night or before passing through a dangerous area.

The observance of certain old rules of good seamanship would have also saved some of these boats, such as choosing one's anchorage carefully, possibly using two anchors in exposed places, checking out the reliability of a mooring cable, or by just leaving a bad anchorage and putting to sea before it was too late. While at Honiara, in the Solomon Islands, at the start of the cyclone season when strong onshore squalls could be expected nearly every day in the exposed anchorage, I became a joke among the other skippers when I religiously left the anchorage and hove to well offshore as soon as a squall approached. Once a freighter broke her moorings, and drifted onto the other boats; another time the winds were so strong that most boats dragged their anchor, yet none of the other skippers left with me and all seemed contented to ride out the squalls at anchor. Yet only a few days after our departure, both the trimaran *Zoom* and a local boat were completely broken up during exactly one of those violent onshore squalls.

Many boats are lost throughout the world for the simple reason that they are in the wrong place at the wrong time of year, yet this is a danger which should be the easiest to avoid. The hurricane or cyclone seasons are well known and sufficient data about tropical storms is now available to allow the prudent navigator to choose a relatively safe area for cruising. Some people, however, still choose to face the risk and continue cruising during the bad season in areas subjected to tropical storms. This decision was fatal for six of the boats included in this analysis, three being lost on passage and three at anchor.

Charmed by two mild hurricane seasons, more than the usual number of boats decided to spend the 1978/79 cyclone season in Fiji, although most of these were cautious enough to stay in the vicinity of proven hurricane holes. After the loss of *Ocean Rover* and *Chimera* during cyclone Meli, nearly every skipper I spoke to the following year was heading out of the area, bound for New Zealand, Australia or Papua New Guinea. Even so, being on the edge of the season myself and worried about it, when I asked the skipper of *Pretender* where he was heading for the hurricane season, I was amazed to receive the reply, 'What hurricane season?' Fortunately, such innocence is rare.

Out of the thirty boats which were wrecked under a variety of circumstances, only five could be said to have been lost as a result of probably unavoidable causes. *Pono* and *Southern Kiwi* were sunk after colliding with unidentified objects at night, *Ponsonby Express* and *Valhalla* vanished at sea when no extreme weather conditions had been reported and their disappearance may never be explained; while the loss of *Pink Mola Mola* could be ascribed to bad luck and nothing else. Luck, whether good or bad, can still play a major part in the safety of our boats. Not for nothing did Willie Willis, the singlehanded raft navigator, maintain that everyone who sets off across the oceans needed an angel on each shoulder. If, besides such heavenly support, one does not leave all watchkeeping to those angels, at the same time paying attention to the accuracy of one's navigation, boat losses could be reduced to a minimum. Unfortunately some of the examples cited seem to point to a low standard of seamanship, but this is a human factor that can be remedied. However, for those who are prepared to approach the sea with prudence and the respect it deserves, and this includes a great deal of serious preparation, a world cruise has every chance of being completed successfully.

THE LOSS OF *MARUFFA*

No one stepping on board *Maruffa* could fail to notice the happy atmosphere among her crew, eight young people always cheerful and full of the joy of living. During a year of cruising together they had cemented their friendships and evolved a tangible communal life. Sitting around the large table in *Maruffa*'s spacious cabin, some of the crew related with relish their adventures sailing *Maruffa* across the Pacific. A quiet young American girl sitting in one corner added a few words and at first I was surprised to find that she was *Maruffa*'s owner, the person who had brought everyone together and created around her such an exceptional atmosphere.

There was always a happy atmosphere on board *Maruffa* among the young crew who sailed her across the Pacific.

Kit Greene had cruised the Pacific before as crew, so when she inherited a considerable sum of money, she knew exactly what she wanted to do. A student of astrology, even the stars at the moment of her inheritance told of a maiden waiting for a sailing boat. Kit was planning to set off with a group of friends on a voyage around the world and now they only needed the boat. She found a Captain in Steve Sewall and together they toured New England looking for her dream boat. It took a long while, but eventually in Maine they discovered *Maruffa*. She was one of Philip Rhodes' classic yachts built in Maine in 1935. She was a 63 ft yawl built of mahogany on oak frames but badly neglected and in need of attention. Designed as an ocean racer and cruiser, she had a fine history behind her as a private yacht cruising the oceans of the world, from the Mediterranean to the Pacific. Later, under Kit Green's ownership, she had been used as a whale research vessel in the North Atlantic by the Woods Hole Oceanographic Institute. In 1976 *Maruffa* took part in the Tall Ships race from Bermuda to Newport and was with the fleet in New York on the 4th July for the 200th anniversary of American Independence.

Maruffa was just waiting for someone like Kit to restore her lovingly to her former glory, while astrology gave Kit the symbol of a winged triangle for her dream boat. By the time *Maruffa* was completely refitted and ready to sail, Kit's friends had gone ahead with other plans, so she had to set about finding a new crew. It wasn't too difficult in New England to find likeable young people, who were game for a world cruise aboard a beautiful sailing boat with all living expenses paid for.

One of Kit's long term plans was to sail to Egypt, led by her star, to pursue her interest in studying ancient astrology. *Maruffa* was even an Arabic name, meaning *The Swift One*. First however she sailed down to the Caribbean, through the Panama Canal and to the Galapagos, where the young crew spent carefree days swimming and diving among the seals and observing the unique wild life on the islands.

Sailing across the Pacific some of the crew changed here and there, but the atmosphere remained the same, with Kit generating a quiet serenity around her. In New Zealand, Kit and her seven friends worked hard for several weeks giving *Maruffa* a major refit; everything was checked and serviced. A new boom and rudder were fitted, wood was scraped, sanded, repainted and revarnished, the eight of them working a daily twelve hour stint. In tip-top condition *Maruffa* then showed her paces in the annual Tall Ships race in the Bay of Islands, before setting off to sail around the southern tip of New Zealand, into Fiordland, and across the Tasman Sea to Australia.

New Zealand's South Island is renowned for its wild weather and lack of shelter, and sailing with a reduced crew of six, *Maruffa* met stormy conditions rounding into the Foveaux Straits. A backstay parted and they decided to run for shelter. Tragedy was poised to strike. Entering a small bay at night, relying on the depth-sounder and radar to grope their way in, they clipped a projecting ledge and the huge seas soon pushed *Maruffa* onto the rocks. It was a black night. In the rough conditions they had difficulty launching the liferafts to get ashore. Trying to rescue one of the liferafts that had been washed overboard, Alex Logan got caught between the side

Maruffa sailing off the New Zealand coast shortly before being wrecked.

of the boat and the rocks and, in moments, the pounding boat severed his leg through completely at the thigh. Another crewman quickly made a tourniquet from his belt and the freezing water helped to staunch the flow of blood. They managed to get ashore with one liferaft and only then did one of the girls realise that she had lost her thumb. Unable to raise anyone on the radio, the crew spent an anxious night huddled on the cliffs inside the liferaft, trying to keep Alex warm and alive. Only when dawn rose could Steve Sewall trek the few miles to the nearest house to raise the alarm, and soon a helicopter had Alex safely in hospital.

Maruffa meanwhile pounded on the rocks, a giant hole in her side. It was impossible to organise a salvage in that remote part of the world, and the sad end for a classic yacht, with forty years of sailing behind her, came quickly.

The Pacific claims many victims every year, and some dreams must end in tragedy. Yet in retrospect Kit feels that the wrecking of *Maruffa* was one of the most crucial experiences of her life.

'It was very much "us" that night, the group rather than the individual, and our emotions were so tangible, as if they had an existence outside as well as inside each of us. I think of other people's tragedies now with a new awareness, and can identify with what they feel. We are all thankful to be alive.'

Out of tragedy came understanding, and Kit Greene still includes sailing among her future plans.

ALBERT STEELE

I almost missed *Peregrine* tucked away in a corner of Nuku'alofa's small port. Battered and stained, the 40-year old cutter did not look all that different from the local boats surrounding it. My eye was caught though, as her white haired owner Albert Steele stepped jauntily ashore, with his Tongan lady Malia on his arm. He wore his 63 years lightly, his tanned and furrowed face pierced by bright blue eyes. After exchanging a few words, it was clear that here was an exceptional man of the sea. Over several evenings of talk on board *Aventura*, I learned of his lifetime of sea-faring adventure and the salty wisdom he had to offer.

Albert has always loved the sea. As a child he used to climb a water tower near his home to watch the square riggers sailing up the Delaware river. He was only twelve years old when he ran away from home and joined a small Bermudan sloop, that dredged for crabs in Chesapeake Bay. The sloop's skipper taught the youngster the art of sailing and even now Albert prefers to steer by points, as he learned that first summer.

Although he returned home in the winter, the saltwater coursing in his veins couldn't be long ignored. The remainder of his teenage years were spent as a deckhand on a variety of sailing boats, seiners fishing off Florida and Texas, coasters trading down the East Coast as far as Maine, and open decked sloops transporting cattle from Puerto Rico to the Virgin Islands. He jumped ship, he stowed away, and rarely hit the same port twice. Vividly he recalls the time he was in Cuba when Batista came to power.

'We were forbidden to leave ship, so of course that was the first thing we did. We found a bar, commandeered all the girls, threw out the locals, locked the door and got steadily drunk on monkey rum, while the guns of the civil war boomed out over Havana.'

He went everywhere, did everything, satisfied every whim. He even served six months on an adult chain gang, though still a juvenile, for stealing a bar of soap.

Peregrine in Nuku'alofa with a notice in Tongan nailed to her mast to keep off uninvited guests.

'It did my physique a lot of good,' he laughs, 'I guess I was a bit of a wild kid in those days.'

After a waterside brawl put twenty stiches in his head, he decided to jump ship in Hawaii. For the next two years he sailed to various Pacific islands on the *Islander*, which had been converted to a fishing boat after its famous ethnological expedition to the islands of Polynesia. In Hawaii he also found time to qualify as a hard hat diver and get his 500-ton master's ticket. He had just turned twenty-one.

Hawaii at this time was beginning to get too 'touristy' for Albert and, undaunted by a seaman's strike which prevented him signing on, he just stowed away on a Navy ship to get himself back to the mainland. He tried working ashore as a rigger for a road show touring California, but the lure of the sea was too strong, so he wound up as first mate on a schooner, fishing the Banks of Campeche in the Gulf of Mexico.

In the late 1930's these snapper schooners were the last stronghold of boats working under sail. All the old salts from the square riggers and sailors from the Grand Banks fleet, had gravitated to that corner of the globe. Aged just 23 Albert got his first command and skippered a crew, the youngest of whom was more than twice his age. They were of all nationalities, but all master seamen, who must have sensed the doom of their trade, for every time they put into port they got hopelessly drunk. Albert rigged his 60 ft schooner so he could manager her singlehanded under jib and staysail. Loading his drunken crew, he would sail her out to the middle of the bay, drop the anchor and wait for them to sober up before they could set sail for the fishing banks.

World War Two sounded the death knell for large scale fishing under sail. Albert, like so many others, was swept up in the great war machine and found himself transported to North Africa and Italy, first as a rigger in a tank recovery unit and then as a salvage diver. After his discharge he returned to Florida, but the sailing schooners had disappeared. Not daunted, he joined the sponge fishing fleet as a diver working off the coast of Florida. The prices for sponges were high and he earned a good $15,000 a year walking on the sea bed. In 1947 sponges from Greece, which had grown untouched during the war years, started flooding the US market. The price dropped dramatically from $35 to $4 a pound and Albert left to look for work elsewhere.

The next chapter in the odyssey took Albert to California, where he studied modern navigation methods and was before long skippering a tuna boat out of San Diego. For years he followed the tuna up and down the Central American coast, to the Galapagos and Ecuador. After a particularly bad storm off Baja California, Albert thought to himself that there must be an easier way to earn a living. So he turned his back on the sea, moved ashore and dedicated himself to something which had always fascinated him, art and antiques.

The other side of his life is evident today in *Peregrine*'s cluttered cabin. A candle in an antique brass stand throws long shadows over shelves crammed with books on period furniture and art history. The bulkheads are hung with old Dutch prints and ancient chronometers. The chart table contains valuable early charts as well as their modern counterparts. It is all that remains of his fine collection of antiques.

During his years ashore, Albert built up a reputation as a specialist in English period furniture. For ten years he refused to even go near the waterfront, but the sea eventually proved the stronger and he satisfied his calling by working part time as a tugmaster.

'I guess I must be the only guy who has given a lecture on 17th century English furniture to a hall full of academics and then ran backstage, put on my overalls and within the hour docked a ship in San Diego harbor. It was an ego trip for me, especially as I never made it past 8th grade at school.' Albert gave one of his infectious chuckles.

'I never had much education, but I've always had a taste for champagne.'

It was a lovely life, he had plenty of money, and had built up a private collection worth quarter of a million dollars. But on the eve of his sixtieth birthday, Albert took a long look at himself and felt life running like sand through his fingers. The saltwater in his veins gave him the answer. He sold a painting and started looking for a boat.

Never a yachtsman, but always a sailor, he had little use for the sleek modern vessels. It took him a long time to find *Peregrine*, a little ship resembling the ones he had sailed in his youth. She matches Albert perfectly; a classic cutter built almost fifty years ago for the Fastnet race of 1936. Built of pitchpine on oak frames, her seven foot bowsprit gives her an overall length of 45 ft. Above and below decks she is simple and functional. The first thing Albert did was to throw out her engine, which he hated with a 'purple passion', then he loaded her up with the remnants of his art collection, now seriously depleted by two divorces, and set forth.

In 1976 he left California bound for Cape Horn and then the Greek Isles. However Albert does not stick to plans. Nor is he a solitary man and had not planned on being a singlehander, it just turned out that way.

At the end of a lifelong involvement with the sea, Albert Steele in the cosy cabin of ageing *Peregrine*.

"I'm just too careful and after my enthusiastic crew had lost a couple of winch handles overboard, I decided to go it alone.' Not only careful, Albert is cautious, tempered by years of experience and knows how to conserve his energy. As a singlehander he often chooses to heave to and rest in broad daylight and good weather, when there is a good chance of his boat being seen by passing ships. He can then rest and stay awake at night or if the weather deteriorates. He is one of the few people who still use a sea anchor, stopping to rest with his double-ended *Peregrine* lying comfortably to a sea anchor streamed from astern.

A trip around the Horn became less and less appealing and making friends on other boats, Albert turned *Peregrine*'s bows west to join the fleet sailing across the Pacific, hoping to find a trace of the atmosphere he had known there more than four decades previously. Tahiti was not at all what he had in mind, but sailing on westward to Tonga he was delighted to find the Polynesian atmosphere he thought had disappeared forever. He decided to stay. As a ticketed captain he is much in demand to skipper local fishing boats, but his plans are only to refit *Peregrine*, sail a little, fish a little, and enjoy the company of pretty Malia.

I met him again in Fiji, where he had gone to have an engine fitted back into *Peregrine*. Pottering in and out of the Tongan reefs in search of shells for a jewellery firm had changed his mind.

With the engine not yet in commission, I towed *Peregrine* from the boatyard in Suva with my dinghy. It was a pleasure to watch the ease and calmness with which he got the 45 footer under sail, every sheet and move carefully synchronised. The weather was miserable, wet and overcast, so it was no surprise to see *Peregrine* still at anchor the next morning, tucked behind the entrance reef to Suva. Albert was in no hurry and I knew he wouldn't take any risks on his trip back through the dangerous Fijian waters to Tonga. Not only singlehanders, but all of us can learn a lot from Albert Steele, sailor from a bygone era.

FOOTNOTE

Shortly before going to press I received the sad news of the loss of yet another of the boats featured in this book, the fifty year old schooner *Hawk*, lost on a reef in the Red Sea. Amateur radio again proved its usefulness in arranging the prompt rescue of the crew.

On March 3rd 1982 Cyclone Isaac swept through the Tongan archipelago causing the loss of several boats spending the hurricane season at Neiafu in the Vava'u group. Out of fourteen cruising boats only four survived with practically no damage, one was sunk and nine were blown ashore and suffered varying amounts of damage. Some of the owners have been able to refloat their boats and undertake the necessary repairs. Cyclone Isaac has again demonstrated that even well sheltered anchorages like Neiafu are not hurricane proof and skippers should be aware of this risk when choosing to remain in such an area during the hurricane season.

CHAPTER FIVE

The Seawives Have Their Say

The Seawives Survey

The sea is in many respects still an area of male supremacy, yet in the field of cruising many notable achievements would not have been possible without female participation. In spite of this, the women's opinion is usually neglected or not even asked for, not just by their skippers, but also by designers, builders, clubs and often boating magazines. While interviewing skippers, I noticed how on several occasions the wife was told more or less politely not to interfere, even in situations where her contribution could have been of value. In all fairness, I should point out that on many other boats the skipper readily consulted his mate on points raised in the survey, while on a couple of boats the skippers were women. After being reproached a few times that my questions seemed to be always directed to the skipper, I was ready to admit that I had nearly committed the same mistake, of passing up blindly the rich source of knowledge and practical experience of the female voyagers.

Out of the total of fifty boats surveyed on practical aspects of seamanship and long distance cruising, forty had a seawife on board. I use the term 'seawife' loosely, as the forty ladies concerned included not only wives, but also girlfriends, mothers and independent women cruising on their own terms. Many of them were experienced sailors in their own right and all of them fulfilled the criteria I had set for the fifty skippers, to have been cruising continuously for at least one year and to have covered a minimum of 5,000 miles away from base. The sample was very representative as it included women of all ages, from early 20's to late 60's, married or single, mothers and grandmothers, divorcees and widows. Their range of occupations and interests were just as wide, farmers and doctors, teachers and nurses, businesswomen and housewives.

Wherever possible I tried to talk to the seawives on their own, but when this was not possible, I firmly asked their skipper not to interfere. In a few cases where the skipper still insisted on butting in, I discreetly ignored him and wrote down the wife's version. Even so, I left the occasional heated argument behind me and was quite happy to get into my dinghy and row away.

Decision to Cruise

For all the 40 seawives who took part in the survey, cruising was a way of life and not just a weekend or holiday pastime. The decision to cut off all ties with a shorebound existence for a life at sea must have been for many of them one of the most radical decisions in their entire life, therefore I asked each of them how much the choice of this way of life had been hers. In 23 cases I was assured that the decision had been mutual, the two partners taking the decision together. In six cases the decision had been taken solely by the skipper, the wife only having the stark choice of accepting it or staying behind. On the other hand, for the five independent women of their own financial means, the decision to go cruising had been entirely theirs. The remaining six gave various percentages to show their participation in the decision making, ranging from 10 to 40 per cent, indicating that in the last resort it had been the skipper's decision that tipped the balance.

'I was blackmailed into it,' said one wife, 'He said he would only marry me if I came with him on a trip around the world in a small boat. So I came.'

The smile with which she said it and the fact that their voyage was one of the longest among those surveyed probably meant that the initial blackmail had turned into a happy memory.

At the other extreme, Denny Bache-Wiig decided to go cruising with her son, thus fulfilling her late husband's lifelong dream. Although not particularly interested in sailing, her husband's plans were so far advanced when he died, that she decided to carry them out herself.

Effects on Marriage

The passive role played by some of the wives in the initial decision to go cruising can lead to serious problems later on, putting in jeopardy not just the continuation of the voyage, but even the marriage itself. Beryl Allmark, who had already been cruising for twelve years with her husband Alan on *Telemark* when I spoke to her, pointed out, 'Cruising is something you either like doing or you don't. There are so many broken marriages among those who set off sailing, because in most cases it was the husband's decision to go and the wife followed only reluctantly.'

My questions on marriage touched on a subject that many women felt very strongly about and most of them were ready to discuss in a frank and forthright manner. Living together in the small confines of a boat while undertaking long ocean passages exerts considerable stresses on any relationship. At the end of a three year long voyage around the world on *Aslan*, Beverly Wilmoth considered the most valuable suggestion she could make to other voyagers was to make sure they could handle being together for long periods at a time. All seawives stressed the importance of a sound marriage, underlining the fact that it was no good taking a shaky marriage to sea. Kathy Becker of *Jocelyn*, summed it up like this: 'The marriage has to be 100 per cent sound for each partner, otherwise it would fall apart.' Kathy is prone to terrible bouts of seasickness in all but the calmest of weathers and suffers a great deal on every passage. Yet she refuses to give up her cruising life, partly because she enjoys the continuous change of scenery and the opportunity to meet new and exciting people, but more importantly because she knows that this is what her husband Jay really wants to do. In her opinion, any amount of physical discomfort is worth taking for the sake of a happy and contented marriage.

The couples who had been cruising for a long time, or who had done a lot of sailing together before their present voyage, certainly seemed to enjoy a

Kathy Becker of *Jocelyn* was one of the many wives who stressed the importance of a sound marriage.

particularly harmonious relationship. The first year of a cruise appeared to be the crucial period in which relationships are tested. Several wives gave examples of voyages abandoned and broken marriages that they had witnessed while cruising. Among the 40 wives surveyed, three have since interrupted their voyage and have returned to life ashore, while their husbands have continued sailing. On the positive side, another two of the women interviewed, shortly afterwards married their skippers, after sailing as equal partners halfway around the world.

The sea is thus a perfect testing ground for marriage, and Karen Huso of *Potpourri* advised potential cruising wives, 'Do some sailing before setting off, so as to make sure that you really want to do it and also that you can live with your husband 24 hours a day.'

Karen Huso scrubs 50 per cent of Potpourri's decks. In the background is the New Zealand boat *Dauntless*, shortly before being rammed and sunk in the South Pacific.

Expectations vs. Reality

Although the primary decision to change their life style was not always theirs, none of the seawives considered that cruising had failed to live up their expectations. In fact, out of 40 seawives, 26 stated that the cruising life was better than they had expected. Six women found cruising very much as they had imagined, neither better nor worse, whereas a further eight admitted that although cruising had lived up to their expectations, they had some reservations. Several of them stated that some aspects were better than expected, while others were certainly worse.

'I like the ports more than I thought I would, and I hate the sailing more than I thought I would. Sometimes I would prefer to see the world by other means,' as Suzanne Hartley of *Tara II* put it.

I was told on several occasions that the rewards of cruising as a way of life were often very different to what the wife had expected before setting off.

'You never get what you think you'll get,' said Jeannette Delvaux of *Alkinoos*. 'That is what makes cruising so challenging. It's definitely not a tourist brochure life, but this is not to say that cruising is not agreeable.' Several wives admitted that they had hoped for a more glamorous life, mostly because their husbands had always talked only about the dreamlike qualities of life on a sailing boat in the balmy tropics. Instead cruising turned out to be much less glamorous, often downright hard and demanding, although some rewards came from unexpected directions. Linda Balcombe of *Starshine* admitted, 'I had a few disappointments, mainly because some of the ideas of what I thought I'd find in the South Pacific were taken from the movies.'

While finding cruising life rewarding in a general way, D'Ann McClain of *Windrose* considered it difficult for an independently minded woman to relinquish most of her freedoms:

'There is less freedom on a boat than one expects. A woman has to be prepared to lose her independence, her autonomy. All the important decisions are taken by the skipper. This can be very frustrating to the wife, because ashore many fundamental decisions are taken by her. The wife often runs the house, but would never run the ship.' As to be expected from a businesswoman, D'Ann knew exactly where she stood and was incensed by the chauvinistic attitudes of many skippers, on whose boats the male played an even more dominating part than on land. On the other hand it was noticeable, especially among the couples who had been sailing for a really long time together, that all important decisions were taken jointly, often the wife dealing with matters which normally are regarded as the province of the skipper.

As in many cases the decision to take up cruising had been initiated by the husband, it was perhaps not surprising that a high proportion of the seawives told me that they had not been really interested in sailing before the plans for the voyage started taking shape. But once the preparations were past the initial stages, most of these seawives began to look at sailing with more enthusiasm. In a few cases the husbands did not have much sailing experience either, so sailing and navigation were learned together.

Generally the break with shore life, family and friends seems to affect women more deeply than men, so I asked all the seawives how much they missed these things. Twenty-two stated that indeed they missed their family, fourteen that they did not and four were undecided or only missed their family on special occasions such as Christmas or Thanksgiving. Most of the women who missed their family were mothers who had never before been separated from their children and grandchildren for long periods of time.

Friends were missed less than family; only 18 women admitted that they missed their friends back home. Several times I was told that the absence of old friends was more than compensated by the new friends made both in the places visited and among other cruising people.

I reached virtually the same conclusions when I brought up this subject again in my survey of the 12 circumnavigators. For instance, Mary-Louise Stewart of *Kyeri* considered the toughest part of the entire voyage was leaving her grown up children behind.

Even less missed than the friends back home were the shore comforts, most of which are denied to those who choose to live on a small boat. Thirty-two of the seawives stated firmly that they did not miss the conveniences of life ashore at all. The eight who missed such comforts did not include any of the women who were on longer voyages, but were drawn from those who had left home recently and for whom these modern conveniences were still fresh in their memories. One thing mentioned by several wives, both among those who missed and those who did not miss their shore comforts, was the shortage of abundant fresh water, which nearly every woman regarded as a great nuisance. Certainly not missed at all was the hardware of a modern home.

'How could I miss them? I've had them all. When you've had a thirteen room house with all the mod cons that go with it, you're glad to be rid of them!'' exclaimed Opal McInness of *Mac's Opal*. Similarly Beverly Wilmoth of *Aslan*, who had been used to a large house with all possible amenities back home.in Texas, found she was quite happy to live and work in the constricted space of a boat with no labour saving devices at all. She had already decided to lead a more simple and modest life when she returned to shore and I was interested to hear from her that in fact they had bought a much smaller house, when they returned from their three year voyage.

It was interesting to note that the longer a woman had been cruising, the

Vicki Holmes was one of the fortunate seawives to have a small washing machine on board *Korong II*.

simpler her life style became. As Susan Hiscock of *Wanderer IV* remarked, 'You just learn to live without these things.' Doing away with some of the machinery of modern living does not mean that all these women lead spartan lives. Many boats are nowadays equipped with freezer or refrigerator, a few have small washing machines and even a microwave oven is not such a rarity any more.

Division of Labour Aboard

Labour division in navigation, boat handling, cooking, washing and most other activities on board played a major part in my survey. On most boats navigation, especially astro-navigation, continued to be regarded as the prime responsibility of the skipper. Twenty-one seawives told me that they never did navigation of any sort, while four did very little. Out of the total of forty, only two wives took care of all the astro-navigation on their boats, the remaining thirteen participated in some measure, on average doing about half the navigation. Among these latter it was more common for the skipper to take the sight and the wife to do the calculations; in most of these cases I was told that the mate had a better way with figures.

Regarding sailhandling, which included raising, lowering and changing sails, as well as reefing, I was somewhat surprised to find that twenty five of the seawives never did any sailhandling at all, a further six did very little and even the proportion of work done by the remaining nine only averaged out at 32 per cent. Only one seawife did all sailhandling herself, admittedly on one of the smaller boats. The size of the boat, and implicitly the size of the sails, was the main inhibiting factor. Muriel Bouteleux of *Calao* even specified·that she regarded a 40 ft boat as the limit for the strength of the average woman.

While most women left the best part of the deck work to their male partners, this does not mean that during sailchanging the wives are just looking idly on, but usually do the necessary work from the cockpit, either handling sheets or being at the helm if the selfsteering or autopilot is disengaged. From a purely statistical point of view, the seawives surveyed did practically as much boat handling as their skippers. Asked to rate as a percentage their share at the helm, both steering while underway and moving in and out of port, twenty one wives rated their helmwork as 50 per cent, the remaining nineteen covered the whole range from 10 to 100 per cent, giving an overall average of 47 per cent.

As the majority of the crew interviewed were couples, seldom taking on additional crew, they had perfected their teamwork, each knowing exactly what to do in a given situation. This was reflected in the precise answers the seawives were able to give me on questions concerning the general handling of the boat. It was particularly noticeable in the question of anchor handling, that those women who normally spent a higher proportion of time at the helm rarely did any anchor work and vice versa. Overall, twenty one wives never handled the anchor, the remaining nineteen doing an average 42 per cent of this work. It was generally on the smaller boats that the women did a higher proportion of the anchor handling or on the larger boats equipped with electric windlasses.

Because of the physical difference between the sexes, a precise allocation of tasks makes sense, although a number of skippers are still reluctant to relinquish the helm. On many occasions I have watched boats coming in to either anchor or to dock with the skipper shouting instructions from the cockpit to a poor woman struggling with several mooring lines or a heavy anchor. Susan Hiscock of *Wanderer IV* made the same point when discussing the division of work on a shorthanded boat:

'Women should know as much as possible about the boat and sailing, so as to take part in the handling of the boat as much as the husband. All things on the boat should be done jointly, yet often the husbands try and make themselves look superior. Coming into congested ports, for instance, the wife should be at the helm and the man at the lines and fending off. It is only vanity on their behalf. They want to be seen to be in control.'

The rest of the questions on labour division were concerned with the domestic chores of cooking, provisioning, washing dishes and clothes. It was these questions which most frequently caused disagreement between skipper and mate, the bone of contention invariably being the percentage of washing up done by either of them. This was the one area of my survey in which my sums hardly ever added up. As on land, the proportion of these chores done by the females was much greater. Fourteen of the wives interviewed did 100 per cent of the cooking, a further five rated their contribution as 95 per cent and fourteen as 75 per cent. In this latter category, the wives cooked the main meals, while the skippers prepared breakfast. On two boats the women did virtually no cooking, but in both cases they did all the navigation. The overall percentage of the cooking done by the seawives interviewed averaged out at 82 per cent.

A similar percentage (83 per cent) of laundry work was done by the wives, although compared to cooking a higher number, twenty two, claimed to do 100 per cent of all washing. There was no wife who did no laundry at all, although on one boat husband and wife did their own washing. Even the independent single girls did a greater percentage than their own personal laundry. The men appeared to help out more with the washing of the dishes, only one quarter of the women claiming to do all the washing up. The remaining thirty seawives did between nil and 90 per cent of the washing up, the average being 68 per cent.

Regarding provisioning, both short and long term, this was definitely a female responsibility. On twenty three boats the wife decided alone all provisioning matters, while on fourteen boats the provisioning was decided jointly.

Several women pointed out that the skippers should not necessarily be always blamed for the traditional division of work along male/female lines. Often it was the woman's fault, for accepting to be cast into a domestic role without protesting. It was a point that Cynthia Hathaway of *Spaciety* felt particularly strongly about. 'A woman should be assertive, should learn how to sail, how to handle the boat. It's no good spending all your time in the galley, because if the man does everything to do with the boat, he naturally expects the woman to do all the housework, like cooking, washing etc.' Muriel Bouteleux of *Calao* entirely shared that opinion. 'All tasks on a boat, from cooking to navigation, should be divided fairly, yet in cooking, laundry or washing up, the same principles seem to operate at sea as on land.' At the time I considered this to be rather wishful advice to other women on Muriel's behalf, as cruising on many occasions in *Calao*'s com-

Muriel Bouteleux trying to find local vegetables to match her French cooking in Papua New Guinea.

pany I had never seen Muriel raise a sail or drop an anchor, but had often enjoyed her delicious French cuisine. On reading this observation in print, Muriel was quite indignant and on all subsequent occasions when we sailed in company, she always made a point of being seen working on deck. Fortunately her cooking did not suffer from this sudden metamorphosis.

In fact, Muriel was one of the eight mothers included in this survey, who were accompanied by their children. Especially in those cases where the children were under the age of ten, a lot of the women's time was occupied with the children, which obviously left them less time for playing a more active role in sailing the boat.

Emergency Competence

Although many of the women interviewed like Muriel did not normally do the sail handling, anchor work or navigation, this did not mean that they did not know how to do these things if necessary. I asked all forty seawives if they could do certain jobs alone in an emergency situation. Thirty eight assured me that they could sail their boat alone if necessary, only two admitting that they were unable to do so, both of these sailing on two of the largest boats in the survey. A much smaller proportion, twenty three out of forty, were confident that they could navigate safely back to a port if the navigator had been incapacitated. Some of the wives who do not normally take part in the navigation of their boat, specified that they had written instructions explaining the step by step procedure for taking and working out of a sight. Nevertheless a surprisingly high number of seventeen women admitted to not being able to do any kind of astro-navigation, not even in an emergency.

Also with an emergency situation in mind, I asked the wives if they could do other specific jobs alone if the necessity arose, such as bringing the dinghy back on board, getting the anchor up, putting to sea from an anchorage, carrying out simple repairs on the engine and setting the self-steering or autopilot. Thirty five women told me that they could bring up the dinghy on their own, while thirty four could cope with the anchor and chain or line. An even higher number, thirty nine, were perfectly able to put to sea on their own, although in many cases I was told that it meant getting the boat underway with the help of the engine. Among the women who could leave an anchorage on their own, those who were unable to lift the anchor back on deck unaided said they would simply leave it behind, possibly buoyed.

Even if practically every one of the seawives knew how to turn the ignition key and, provided the engine started, could get the boat moving, the engine itself remained a mystery for most women. Only six wives were confident enough that they could carry out at least some simple repairs on their engine. My test question was to ask them whether they knew how to purge their diesel engine if air had entered the fuel system. Although it is one of the commonest reasons why a diesel engine may stop running, thirty two women admitted that they could not cope with such a problem.

Setting the automatic pilot seemed to present less difficulties and all six women whose boats were equipped with autopilots knew how to use them. Three boats had no selfsteering device whatsoever, whereas on the remaining thirty one boats equipped with wind operated selfsteering gears, twenty seven of the seawives were able to set them, only four being unable to do so.

Those women who were not capable of doing some or most of these jobs alone were aware of their shortcomings and regretted not having become more proficient at sailing before setting off. In fact, it was mostly these less experienced seawives, who suggested that any woman contemplating a long distance cruise would be well advised to try and learn as much as possible about sailing before setting off, as this would not only make their life easier later on, but would also put them on an equal footing with their male partners.

The possibility of the skipper becoming totally or partially incapacitated while on passage is very real and the reluctance of many skippers to delegate any responsibility to their crew can have grave consequences. This survey has shown that on several boats not only was the skipper in total command, but also that the precautions taken to cope with certain problems in his absence were often inadequate. There are several examples of the crew being forced to cope on their own after the skipper had been put out of action, one of the most poignant being that of a boat on passage from Hawaii to American Samoa. Several days after leaving Hawaii, the skipper, who was in his sixties, collapsed. Up to that moment he had kept a regular schedule with an amateur radio network, so his wife was able to call up the same frequency and request help, It soon became obvious that she had no idea how to sail or handle the boat, work out a position or even start the engine to charge up the batteries when these started getting flat. Eventually the US Coastguard was forced to send out a plane to parachute a doctor and navigator in the vicinity of the stricken boat. They gave emergency treatment to the skipper and sailed the boat to the nearest island, from where the patient was airlifted back to Hawaii. The very real danger of this kind of emergency occurring on a boat in mid-ocean came to me forcefully during a passage from Sri Lanka to Aden, when for two days I was knocked out by a severe bout of malaria. Fortunately the crew of *Aventura* managed perfectly on their own, showing me that at least on my own boat the skipper was not indispensable.

The Right Age for Cruising

Thirty five of the seawives considered their present age to be a good age for this kind of life. The forty women interviewed included eight in the 20–30 age group, nineteen in the 30–40 group, five between 40 and 50 years old, while eight were over 50. The only group where opinion was divided on this subject was among the over 50's, five of whom considered their age as right, while three regretted not having been able to have gone cruising earlier in life. Ilse Gieseking of *Lou IV*, who took a few years off from her business to fulfil her dream of sailing around the world, explained why it would have been better to have gone cruising at a younger age:

'Starting younger would be better, then one could go around the world three times. Now I have only enough time left for twice. In my next life, if I have a choice, I'll do the sailing first and work later.' But Denny Bache-Wiig of *Rising Sun*, who is in the same age group as Ilse Gieseking, told me that, 'It's a fine age of course, especially as I've never gone past eighteen in my own mind.'

Derry Hancock took motherhood in her stride and before baby Tristan was six weeks old, he had successfully completed a 1000 mile passage from Fiji to New Zealand.

At the other end of the age scale, the only young person to have reservations about the right age for cruising was Derry Hancock of *Runestaff*, who had her first baby in Suva, during their cruise:

'Perhaps it would be better to be a bit older and know where you are going, and also what you really want to do with your life.'

As their partners' interest in sailing appeared to have been primarily responsible for these women's new way of life, I asked all seawives if they would again consider marrying a sailor, or a person interested in sailing. I also asked those who were not married if they would consider it. Twenty nine of the wives replied in the affirmative, four gave a very firm *no*, and a further four gave some qualifications, such as 'I'd only marry a sailor if he had plenty of money.' In the remaining three cases the question did not seem suitable, so it was not asked. The four women who said that they would not marry a sailor, all stated that if they had the choice again, they would definitely not marry at all.

'I wouldn't marry again for all the tea in China,' said one of these women and it was interesting to note that on her own boat, the division of domestic chores was absolutely fair, down to each of them doing their own laundry. She certainly meant what she said. Among those willing to accept the role of a sailor's wife again, and they formed the majority of the sample, one woman was candid enough to admit that she would probably make the same mistake again.

The change of life style and environment had certainly affected these women more than their male partners and this was probably the reason why throughout the interviews they tended often to make general comments, not relating just to themselves but to other seawives as well. Some of these comments, concerning marriage or the sharing of work, have been quoted earlier.

Suggestions for Others

At the end of each interview I asked the seawives if they wished to make some practical suggestions for the benefit of other women who intend to follow their example and set off on a long voyage. Dottie Fletcher, who both in port and at sea always has her hands full looking after her large family on board *Duen*, or helping with the maintenance work of this demanding boat, struck a realistic note when she advised potential seawives, 'Try and do some sailing even before you decide on buying a boat, it's a life you either love or you don't. There is nothing in between.'

Although most seawives appeared to accept quite happily the absence of most conveniences of a modern home, some insisted on having at least a few basic comforts. Nancy Payson of *Sea Foam* was among these, and advised 'Try and have some comforts on your boat that are not too complicated. One spends so much time in the galley that one should try and have as many conveniences there as possible, like an oven, two sinks and, most importantly, a narrow and secure galley.'

Alice Simpson of *Fawn of Chichester*, an English girl fond of her cup of tea, pointed out that 'when cruising one spends in fact more time at anchor than at sea, so one shouldn't worry too much about breakable things, as it is so much nicer to drink out of ceramic mugs or glasses than plastic beakers.'

Several seawives stressed the importance of having their own interests and hobbies. Helga Seebeck, who had sailed around Cape Horn in the company of two male friends on the catamaran *Shangri-La*, insisted on her full share of all responsibilities on board. Her suggestion was 'Have another hobby besides sailing, that is, if sailing was your hobby in the first place.'

Brita Zeldenrust of *Kemana* was even more precise when she said 'Wives should have a hobby of their own; macramé, painting, fishing, studying birds, music, collecting shells, ham radio or writing. If such an interest is served by sailing or cruising, the better for it.'

Many of those interviewed took their hobbies very seriously or in the case of Kathy Becker of *Jocelyn*, her passion for amateur radio helped her put up with severe seasickness on long passages. Some suggestions were of a more practical nature, such as the one made by Barbara Dewey of *Hawk*: 'Acquire cookery books from the various countries. Try and cook dishes from strange places, otherwise you get tired of the same menu.' 'Stock up with good reference books on the places you intend to visit,' advised Alice Simpson of *Fawn of Chichester*, 'as these are not always available in the places themselves.'

Rather than give suggestions, some women preferred to make a general comment on their present way of life, which, they hoped, could be of use to other women. 'A seawife is not a housewife afloat,' commented Stefani Stukenberg of *Orplid*, 'because on a boat the two partners depend so much more on each other. This is something a woman should consider carefully

Stefani and Rolf Stukenberg in happier days in Fiji before losing their *Orplid* on the Great Barrier Reef.

beforehand, as she is going to lead a life totally different from that ashore. On board she will never be just a wife.'

Even some of those wives who said that cruising had lived up to or even exceeded their expectations, were quick to point out the often unpleasant side of cruising and the danger of setting off with preconceived ideas. 'Don't think it is suburban life, because it isn't. You may have to get up to 3 am when the anchor drags,' was the sobering comment made by Beryl Allmark of *Telemark*. 'Be ready to make your sacrifices, never to have your hair and nails done, and generally to be forced to work harder than at home,' said Kay Malseed of *Macushlah*, who nevertheless always managed to look smart and attractive.

But in spite of many disadvantages, as those mentioned by Kay or Beryl, several seawives emphasised that in the long run all these sacrifices were worthwhile.

This is how cruising life was summed up by Nancy Lewis of *L'Orion*.

'People who have given up cruising were often those who were expecting this life to be something extraordinary. In fact, it is not extraordinary at all, just fantastically ordinary.'

It was also Nancy who suggested that many wives' frustrations started from small things, such as not having their own dinghy and that often a female's independence should start with her insistence on having at least a small standby inflatable dinghy with which to go ashore when she felt like it.

In the end, what counted more than anything else appeared to be the wife's mental attitude, which was summed up by Marg Miller of *Galatea IV*, 'Prepare yourself mentally, as it is very important to have a positive attitude to this kind of life.'

Ilse Gieseking of *Lou IV* was one of those who never had any doubts about the beauty of cruising life and when I asked for her suggestions she replied, 'If I gave some really good suggestions, the world's oceans would get overcrowded. If people only knew how beautiful this life can be, they would all set off, but they are too afraid.'

The overall conclusion I reached from my lengthy discussions with these seawives, several of whom have an outstanding record of ocean cruising behind them, is that the cruising life has innumerable rewards that far outweigh the inherent discomforts of life afloat. This observation is born out by the fact that most of the crews included in this survey planned to carry on cruising as long as possible, while many of those who were returning for various reasons to a land based existence, were already planning their next voyage. Most of these regarded settling back ashore with some trepidation. In many respects the sea had shown them what was truly essential in life, and this they often proposed to apply to their shorebound lives.

For a woman who takes up cruising as a way of life, the changes from a landbound existence are often greater than for a man, as are the mental and physical adaptations demanded of her. I certainly feel that if the man on board is aware of these demands and shows more understanding of the woman's different physical and mental makeup, the voyage stands a much better chance of success. Many men would do well to heed the sound advice of circumnavigator Herb Stewart of *Kyeri*, whose catchphrase for a successful cruise is 'Keep your wife happy.'

Two Voyaging Women

ILSE-MARIE GIESEKING

Many women participate fully in cruising and none more so than Ilse-Marie Gieseking, known as Illa to her many friends. I would even be so bold as to say that she was the driving force behind *Lou IV*'s successful circumnavigation. Illa always plays her full part in decision taking, route planning and does a considerable amount of the navigation. Like many couples who have sailed together for many years, the boatwork on *Lou IV* is

Illa and Herbert Gieseking with their much loved friend Joshua Slocum.

evenly divided and runs smoothly, usually Illa being on the helm and Herbert on deck.

Many of the sailing wives I encountered were novices, but not Illa, for she has been sailing for over thirty years. The Giesekings have owned several boats previously, and sailing out of Elmshorn in Northern Germany over the years, they have cruised in the Baltic and the North Sea, visiting Scandinavia, the Orkneys and Shetland islands, Scotland and England. But these trips satisfied them less and less and the temptation of a circumnavigation, something they had always dreamed of, became unbearable.

Illa was well used to making decisions, as for years she had run the business side of a small family firm, started by her grandfather, that made doors and window frames. She came to an agreement with her brother to look after things, while she took off a few years for her dream cruise. Everything was so well organised on board *Lou IV*, that the voyage was bound to be a success. The 31 ft fibreglass ketch designed in Denmark by Jensen, was surprisingly roomy and well organised for its length, even having an aft cabin, although that was rather too hot and airless for the tropics. No job was ever postponed on *Lou IV* and the boat was impeccably maintained, returning home after four and a half years and 46,000 miles with all original sails and hardly a scratch on the topsides.

Sailing a boat in tip-top condition and with their long experience, it is not surprising that the voyage exceeded Illa's expectations. Although following the normal trade wind route, or as Illa calls it 'the route of least resistance', they did however make some notable detours. The longest was to sail the entire eastern seaboard of the United States to Canada, up the St Lawrence river into the Great Lakes and back down the Eyrie barge canal and Hudson river to New York. They were also one of the few cruising boats to venture south and cruise off New Zealand's South Island. In Illa's opinion that was the toughest cruising they had ever experienced, worse than the North Sea with wild weather, strong currents, and deep anchorages where the wind screamed down the mountains. The lonely grandeur of the scenery was the only compensation. Apart from a soft spot for Moorea, Illa's favourite cruising ground was the Solomon Islands, which she found to be unspoilt and little visited by tourists or yachts.

Illa's constant companion on the cruise was a small black poodle called Joshua Slocum. Although she loves him dearly and finds him a great pleasure at sea, she admits it was a mistake taking him with them, for it restricted their visits ashore in many places. Illa's warm expansive character extended to children too, as mine were quick to discover and exploit, as Illa never failed to produce a piece of chocolate when they paid her a visit.

Reluctantly the Giesekings turned *Lou IV*'s bow back from the Pacific towards Europe, for Illa could not leave her brother holding the fort for too long. Then tragedy struck them, their only son being killed in a road accident in Germany, unbeknown to them while they were on the long passage from Capetown to the Azores. Illa now had lost any interest she had in keeping the business going. Life ashore suddenly seemed hollow, with nothing to work for and no one to pass on to. She also found that the years at sea had changed her and she now had a different attitude to life than the people around her. What had seemed important before no longer mattered.

There were pleasures on their return home, seeing old friends and a splendid welcome by their yacht club. They also received the Kronenkompass, the highest cruising award of the Germany Cruising Club. In her typical efficient way, Illa wrote, published and sold her own book of their cruise. The pleasures however soon began to pall and there was only one solution as far as Illa was concerned, to leave again and this time for as long as she and Herbert were physically able. Now she is folding up her share of the family business and selling her property. *Lou IV* is already sold and *Lou V* well on the way to completion, a forty ft steel ketch built to the Gieseking's specifications by a small Danish firm of boatbuilders. Illa has a poster of Moorea on her wall, to remind her in the grey German winter of tropical beaches and sunshine, and she also has a large calendar, where she ticks off the number of days left until their planned departure in 1984, this time forever.

DENNY BACHE-WIIG

Following their dreams would aptly describe most world cruising people, but Denny Bache-Wiig is more unusual as the dream she is following is not her own. Denny is an attractive lady of uncertain age (although never past eighteen in her own mind). She readily admits to having five children over the age of twenty one. A few years ago she could be found teaching in Arizona, running a craft shop and learning craft and jewellery techniques from the Indian tribes of Arizona. A complete landlubber, the sea had never interested her. Her husband Ted, on the other hand, had always been keen on sailing and was planning a cruise to Japan on his yacht. Fate intervened however, a terminal cancer struck swiftly and he was never to realise his dream. Denny found herself suddenly not only a widow, but the owner of a 37 ft Lapworth designed sloop *Rising Sun*, fitted out for world cruising complete with the Aries selfsteering gear.

The obvious thing was to sell *Rising Sun*, but Denny felt that would have been a betrayal of Ted. She thought that there must be something in the sea and sailing to have so fascinated her late husband. It so intrigued her that she became determined not to sell the boat, but to live out Ted's dream for him.

Having no knowledge whatsoever about sailing, she enrolled in a navigation class at night school, while her youngest son Danny, who had not originally planned cruising either, studied and prepared to become *Rising Sun's* skipper. Within a year, equipped with a lot of book knowledge, but little practical experience, the two of them set sail from Los Angeles bound for Hawaii, with another couple of Denny's children as additional crew. After a pleasant 21-day passage, Denny proudly provided them with a perfect landfall.

Mother and son, the Bache-Wiigs in New Zealand after their successful cruise from California.

To her amazement Denny discovered that she actually enjoyed sailing, was little affected by seasickness and with all her children grown up, found that it was a perfect age for a footloose and fancy free life. She was hooked. Her original plan had been just to sail to Japan and look for a teaching job there, but on becoming a sailor she soon discovered that plans can easily be changed. Talking to other voyagers she decided it might be interesting to visit New Zealand and so mother and son turned *Rising Sun*'s bows for Samoa, Tonga, Fiji and New Zealand.

The Bache-Wiigs have some savings but not a lot of money, so they are pleased when they can earn some money along the way. Denny's interest in craft also helps with the finances. She ran a craft shop for some time in Hawaii, while in Whangarei, she set up her own stall in the local market, making and selling silver and turquoise jewellery to original North American Indian designs, also weaving the colourful 'Ojo de Dios' or 'God's Eyes', of brightly coloured wool, another skill learned from Arizona's Indians. *Rising Sun*'s cabin is brightly decorated with Denny's work and various carvings bought en route, while she herself brightens the waterfront in distinctive clothes worn with her own indian jewellery.

Denny believes the 'Ojos de Dios' bring her luck. She has not been lacking it so far. Japan is still her ultimate goal, but being in no hurry, it will be a while before she gets to the land of the Rising Sun, there being many interesting places to visit on the way. Following a borrowed dream, Denny has discovered for herself the pleasures of sailing.

CHAPTER SIX

Cruising with Children

Children on cruising boats are no longer the exception, as more and more families, who undertake long voyages, take their children with them. Cruising with children does present certain problems however, and in my second survey of long distance cruising boats one section dealt exclusively with questions concerning children. Out of fifty boats, eight had children on board, and I also questioned a ninth boat, on which the 17-year old was already playing a full part as an adult member of the crew. On five boats the children were single, the remaining four having two children each. The ages varied from three to seventeen, the majority being in the eight to thirteen year old group.

Growing Up Afloat

With only one exception, all parents considered that their children's general attitude to life at sea was good, some describing it as perfect or pointing out that, as the children had virtually grown up at sea, they took boat life for granted, regarding it as the normal thing. Children seem to adapt much more easily than adults to living in a water environment and this perhaps was the reason why heavy weather did not bother most of the children, many carrying on with their activities as in normal weather. Several parents mentioned that during bad weather children went to sleep and slept soundly through anything, although sometimes taking to the main cabin floor, especially when their normal bunks were in the foc'c'sle.

The only parents with some reservations were those of the youngest children, three and five years old at the time of the survey, who did get sick and miserable for short periods during heavy weather. The parents did find however, that their children's attitude to life at sea was getting progressively better as they grew older. Vicki Holmes of *Korong II* admitted that it was a strain cruising with two small children, but she hoped that it would improve when the children were old enough to give the parents some time to call their own and it was not necessary to permanently watch what the children were up to. After a two year cruise, Vicki and John Holmes did return home, although they are determined to set off again as soon as the children reach a more convenient age. Olga and Benoit Soulignac of *Chloe* encountered a similar problem with their young twins, so they interrupted their world voyage for a few years in Tahiti to give the children a chance to grow up before carrying on.

Another couple with a child in this pre-school age group was Sylvia and Ian French of *Pomona* among the dozen circumnavigators I interviewed later. Keeping young John occupied and amused took up most of the parents' time, both in port and on passage.

Occupying older children while on long passages was easier, with reading being the favourite pastime. Most cruising children read a lot, one of them

Toby and James helped considerably with sailing *Duen*.

devouring a book almost every day. Obtaining an adequate supply of reading material, especially in smaller places was often a major problem, although the children themselves often overcame this by swapping books with those on other boats. Games and puzzles were also popular, two children close in age played a great deal together, while one solitary child did a lot of drawing and appeared contented to live in his own imaginary world.

, All the children helped out with jobs to a lesser or greater extent, even five year olds doing simple things like tidying up and coiling ropes. Eight year olds would progress to washing up or handling the jib sheets in normal weather. All the children over eleven participated fully in life aboard, some of them being given precise jobs, while others helped out generally. All the older children also stood watches when at sea. Two children, aged eight and ten, on different boats, had to do an hour watch in the daytime. The five children between the ages of eleven and thirteen all stood full daylight watches. On *Fortuna*, Paul and Tina Morrish, thirteen and eleven at the time of the survey, had been keeping full watches for some time and as the boat had no selfsteering, they had to steer by hand day and night, whatever the weather. On *Sea Foam*, seventeen year old Craig had been taking a full day watch from the age of ten and also a night watch from the age of fourteen.

In every case the children living afloat did appear to be mature and responsible for their age. Linda Balcombe of *Starshine* pointed out that her eleven year old daughter Heather had matured considerably compared with her peer group as a result of living in an adult world. 'I think it is a good life for these children, they see a lot of the world and it can't help but be an improvement.'

Education

These watchkeeping children would appear to have little time for boredom, as they also had to cope with school work and correspondence courses. Education is one of the major concerns of all parents taking their children out of the school system for any length of time and none of those surveyed had neglected this aspect. Nearly all the children were using a correspondence course from their country of origin, which meant that it would be easier for them to rejoin their particular system if and when they returned ashore later on.

The Calvert School correspondence course was used on four American boats, which they all found to be satisfactory. Only one parent qualified this praise by saying that although the system was good for the basic skills at a lower age, she had some reservations about the later grades and particularly the science subjects needed supplementing. Another parent, who considered the Calvert excellent value at the price of $150 per grade, chose, however, not to send the work back for correction.

The return of completed work for correction was one of the major problems encountered by all those using correspondence courses, as reliable mailing addresses were rare and the mailing of material to and from remote places was erratic and unpredictable. The children had often forgotten about the work by the time it arrived back with marks and comments, which was especially true in the case of younger children. This was a particular bugbear for the yacht *Calao*, who used the state system provided free by the French government. As schooling of French children is compulsory, regardless of where they are, it meant that a large amount of work had to be sent back regularly, the rigid requirements of the scheme being a great strain on both the children and their parents. Several times they had to delay their departure from a port, waiting for new course work to arrive. As well as being rigid, they found the system very difficult to adapt to the cruising way of life.

This was also a criticism levelled at some of the Australian and New Zealand courses, which had been written with children on remote sheep stations and farms in mind, and contained such directives as 'go outside and run around the paddock.' The course provided by the Australian state of Queensland received excellent marks as one of the best correspondence courses available and it was used on many boats, not only those from Queensland.

One crew had solved the problem of both the relevance of the material and the marking of it, by devising their own system of education. Liz MacDonald of *Horizon*, who is a qualified teacher, educated her son Jeff entirely by herself during their three year long circumnavigation. Liz tried hard to keep the material relevant, for example in Fiji, where I spoke to her, she was teaching from a book of Pacific history used in the local schools. Throughout the voyage, Liz conscientiously kept an exact record of all the work, Jeff's behaviour and attitude, as well as his marks. She found it essential to stick to a daily routine and definite timetable, an absolute requirement also pointed out by other teaching parents. The discipline involved in educating children at sea was considered by many parents as one of the most trying and difficult aspects of cruising.

It is no wonder then that many parents happily sent their children off to local schools whenever a stay in port was long enough to warrant this. On the other hand, two boats using the Calvert system never sent the children to school ashore, so as not to interrupt the course unnecessarily, while the children on another boat only went to school in English speaking countries. Some parents however used the chance offered by travelling in foreign lands for their children to learn another language. This is why Sidonie and Fabien of *Calao* speak English with a broad Australian accent and my own children used to speak French with a Polynesian twang picked up after one month of school on Mangareva in French Polynesia.

Another reason some parents gave for sending their children to local schools was the chance to make contact and mix with children of their own age. Some of the sailing children made friends only slowly with children ashore, although more easily with children on other boats. About half of the children however, who had got used to their peripatetic life, had learned to make friends at lightning speed, knowing that time was short and soon they would be on the move again.

As the children progress into teenage, this need for friends of similar age becomes more acute and their schooling also gets increasingly difficult. Several of these families planned to end their cruise before their children got too old and were thinking of staying ashore for a few years while the children completed their education. The thirteen year old on one of the boats surveyed was eventually dispatched home to attend school. Other boats with children on board which I have met over the years, but were not included in this survey, had run into similar problems. After using correspondence courses for a while, one French couple decided to send their two teenage children home to boarding school, aiming to cruise in convenient places where the children could join them during their holidays. Neither parents nor children were too happy with this arrangement, so after a year the boat was sold in Singapore, the cruise abandoned and the entire family returned to France. A New Zealand couple also found it very difficult to get their teenager to apply himself to school work and eventually sent him home ahead of them. Unfortunately the parents found that he never caught up with his age group and left school discontented and with a feeling of inferiority.

Most of the points raised here I know only too well from personal experience, my children Doina and Ivan being seven and five when we left England and thirteen and eleven when we returned six years later. Like Liz MacDonald, my wife Gwenda qualified as a teacher as part of the long term preparations for our cruise, and devised a personal education for our children. They studied Greek history and legends in the Aegean, the Bible stories in Israel, the history of the slave trade in the West Indies and discussed Thor Heyerdahl's theories on the way to Easter Island. Whenever possible we sent the children to school ashore, even for as little as two

Gwenda Cornell supervising Ivan's school work, while repairing a sail. Supervising children's education was a demanding task for the cruising parents.

days as on Pitcairn Island. We found schools everywhere to be very welcoming and friendly and their teachers seemed to value the window on the outside world that Doina and Ivan were able to open to the children in such remote communities.

We had originally planned to be back on land for their secondary education, but we all enjoyed life afloat so much that our cruise was extended. As Doina reached thirteen, Gwenda found it more and more difficult to cope with teaching all subjects and she subscribed to correspondence courses from the National Extension College in Cambridge. Although designed primarily for adults, the courses seemed perfectly suited for an older child, as much of the work was self-marked and the assignments did not have to be sent back to the tutor too frequently, a great advantage for the student continually on the move. On returning to England after more than six years afloat we were pleased to find that the children had no problems with their schooling and in fact had a great richness of experience and general knowledge to draw on. They did however experience some difficulty fitting in socially at school, partly because they were not used to school life and also stood out as being slightly different.

Taking children out of the system and educating them afloat is perfectly possible, but does require a great amount of effort, patience and above all discipline, both from parents and children. Gwenda regards schooling as being by far the most demanding and time consuming aspect of our voyage, a point of view shared by most parents. It is the price one has to pay.

Sylvia and Ian French, who left with son John aged twenty months on a three year long circumnavigation on *Pomona*, planned to be back home by the time John was due to start school. On their return however they did not regard this aspect to be as crucial as they had originally thought, and would consider taking him out of school if they made another voyage.

Infants Aboard

Schooling may be headache to many parents, but having toddlers on board is not easy either, as they require constant supervision and the parents cannot properly relax until the child can swim. At the bottom end of the scale, small babies thrive quite happily in the salty atmosphere of a rocking boat. Derry Hancock of *Runestaff* gave birth to Tristan in Suva at the time of my first survey and at the age of only six weeks Tristan made the 1000 mile passage to New Zealand quite happily, although the Hancocks did take an extra crew to give them a hand. Water babies suddenly seemed the fashion, as several cruising boats increased their crews the following year. This often raised the question of the new arrival's nationality and passport, and the new parents had variable amounts of difficulty trying to sort out this problem with their respective embassies.

None of the parents sailing with children regretted their decision to take the family with them to sea. Many mentioned that it brought about a closeness in their family life, which they had rarely experienced before. It was also pointed out that the fathers were far more involved with bringing up their children than when the family had been living ashore, with the father only seeing the children for a few hours a day, whereas on a boat the family was together all the time. The presence of children also guaranteed a warmer reception in most communities and even officials visiting a boat tended to be more friendly when children were about.

While none of the parents regretted taking their children to sea, the

Cruising as a family has many rewards, not least the friendly reception people everywhere give to children. Jimmy, Gwenda, Doina and Ivan Cornell in the South Pacific.

children themselves had little choice in the matter. Some of the older children however were not too happy about living in such a close family environment and had more reservations about life afloat than their parents. From views expressed by both children and parents it would appear that family cruising is more successful before the children reach adolescence.

CHAPTER SEVEN

Long Term Planning

A long and successful ocean cruise is invariably the result of careful planning. Sometimes it takes years to arrange all aspects of shore life so that it is finally possibly to cast off. However, it is by no means always true that exact routes and schedules must be adhered to slavishly: one of the virtues of good cruise planning is to allow for flexibility and improvisation if necessary. Unexpected delays and diversions can occur, and the true meaning of good planning is therefore preparation for a variety of options. The truth of this is well underlined by the experiences of two boats I encountered during my own circumnavigation – the MacDonalds on *Horizon* and the Bouteleux on *Calao*. Their stories are both object lessons in different ways, and on the following pages a brief outline follows:

The MacDonald's Five-year Plan

Life in rural New England for Bruce MacDonald was dull, as he struggled to support his wife Liz and baby son Jeff on a ski-instructor's income. He avidly read true adventure stories, whether mountain climbing or deep sea diving, polar expeditions or safaris across Africa. The books only made it worse for the young couple and the future seemed as bleak and dull as the present. Climbing Mount Everest or trekking to the North Pole looked impossible, but to sail away across the oceans was one dream they felt might be possible to fulfil one day. They drew up a five year plan and that alone injected a new purpose and challenge into their daily routine.

Reading every book they could find about sailing and ocean cruising, the MacDonalds started planning. They soon realised that the first require-ment was a good reliable boat and raising the capital for that was their biggest hurdle. So the young couple put their five year plan into action. They both took better paid teaching jobs and started saving. To raise the capital they set about building a house in their spare time, doing all the building, carpentry, plumbing and heating themselves, hoping that the eventual sale of the house would provide the funds for their boat.

MAP F Most popular routes for circumnavigators taking advantage of prevailing winds

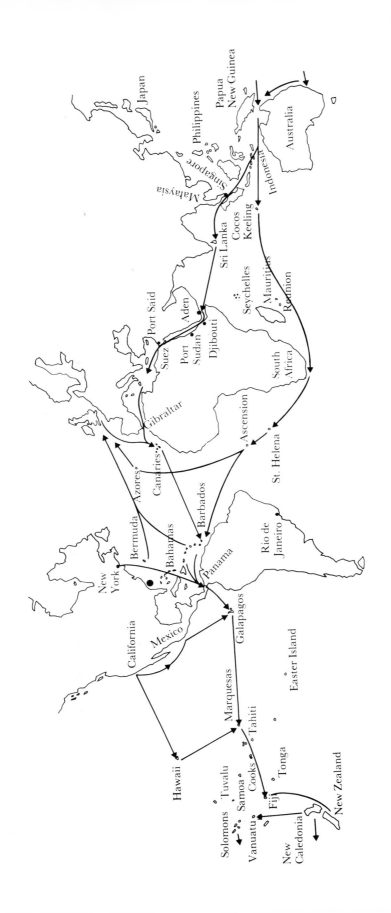

To learn about sailing they acquired a 14 ft sailing dinghy, which they took on long trips to Lake Champlain. Bruce had learned navigation and much about the sea as watch officer on a destroyer in the US navy during his military service, so at least in one province they did not have to start from scratch.

Meanwhile they worked and saved every cent, although often they had serious doubts that their dream would ever become a reality. Then in 1977, they sold everything they possessed and were able to buy *Horizon*, a second-hand Golden Hind sloop. That still left them enough savings over to live modestly for a few years afloat. The 31 ft Golden Hind was the best boat they could afford and they regarded the fibreglass sheathed plywood hull as sturdy enough to take them across the oceans.

I first met the MacDonalds in Beaufort, North Carolina, while they were waiting for a break in the weather to embark on their first long ocean passage. It is difficult for novices, let alone for experienced skippers, to judge the right moment to leave from the United States for the Caribbean. An early departure means running the risk of a late hurricane or tropical depression, while the later it gets into winter, the greater the chance of strong northerly gales which, blowing against the three knot current of the Gulf Stream, chop up treacherous swell conditions. I left in early November and had to skirt a tropical depression, fortunately tracked accurately by the US weather bureau, whereas the MacDonalds' later passage to Puerto Rico tested their endurance to the utmost. With constant northerlies of 40 knots and over, they broke gear, blew out the mainsail and nearly lost their mast. In Puerto Rico they discovered that the mast had compressed and buckled nearly four inches at the base and had to be unstepped, cut and re-fitted. However, they were not daunted by their rough baptism and carried on with their plan of cruising the Caribbean, telling themselves that these were all unavoidable teething problems caused by their lack of experience and hasty preparations. Bruce and Liz soon discovered that the cruising life exceeded their expectations and that in spite of all difficulties it was worth carrying on. The possibility of a world voyage had always been in the back of their minds, so they took the plunge. They went through the Panama Canal and headed west.

Bearded Bruce is as tall as petite Liz is tiny, but both agree that cruising has brought a closeness to their family life. Bruce feels that for son Jeff to see his parents coping with real stress situations only benefits a child and they have had their share of those, such as when Liz had to be hoisted up the mast at sea to replace a broken halyard.

As both parents are qualified teachers, they opted to teach Jeff themselves, although this became mainly Liz's duty. In her thorough way she

The MacDonalds on *Horizon* proved that determination can make anything possible.

applied herself to this mammoth task with great discipline, teaching Jeff the history and geography of all the places visited. Using the environment of tropical vegetation and coral reefs provided nature study, whilst they kept his mathematics up to scratch. She kept a meticulous record of everything she did and made sure that no aspect of Jeff's education was overlooked.

Their budget had to be equally meticulous, as their limited savings meant they had to plan and watch every cent. With inflation and rising prices the budget got tighter and tighter as the voyage progressed. At least a chance of work in New Zealand allowed them to replace *Horizon*'s doubtful mast before crossing the Indian and Atlantic oceans. Their tight budget did not stop them enjoying life and following their particular hobby of walking and mountaineering. They trekked across many of the islands on foot, the high impenetrable Marquesas being one of their favourite places.

In 1980 after sailing 34,000 miles, they had the great satisfaction of accomplishing what they had set out to do, to circumnavigate the globe. The MacDonalds are for me the best example to be given to all those who say 'Aren't you lucky', for they have shown how much hard work, determination and planning are needed. And how little depends on being lucky.

Like many parents who would prefer to remain afloat but cannot do it, Bruce and Liz have settled ashore until teenage Jeff has finished his education, but a new plan is already taking shape. Like other circumnavigators, Bruce would like a steel cutter for his next boat, hoping to buy the hull and fit it out himself in his backyard. The MacDonalds have already set their sights on 1986 for their departure date on an indefinite cruise. With their determination, I have no doubts they will fulfil this plan too.

Rendez-vous with Calao

It began quite early in our circumnavigation of the world. A blonde fellow of my own age was watching us from the cockpit of his boat, as we edged *Aventura*'s stern towards the Yacht Club wall after having dropped anchor in Santa Cruz de la Palma. Seeing all the other boats had a stern line to the wall, I started preparing a long line to take ashore.

'If you desire my dinghy, you can have her!' I heard the chap shout across from his boat.

'No, thanks, I have to launch mine anyway,' I replied, trying to suppress my amusement at his unintentional *double entendre*.

'I'll come and aid you,' he said with a brilliant smile, and without waiting for a reply, jumped into the object of my rejected desire and with a hefty shove brought himself alongside *Aventura*.

'I am Erick Bouteleux . . . from France,' he added, unnecessarily, as from his unmistakable accent I had already guessed that he could not possibly hail from anywhere else.

So started a long friendship between our two crews, nurtured by countless hours of cockpit chatter under balmy tropical skies, joint spearfishing or fruit gathering expeditions for Erick and I, exchange of schooling and cooking tips between Muriel and Gwenda, and ear-splitting discussions in atrocious franglais between Sidonie, Fabien, Doina and Ivan, while *Calao* and *Aventura* reeled off thousands of miles cruising in company.

We met again in Barbados, where *Calao* arrived after an excellent crossing of only eighteen days from the Canaries, which however had been beset by a series of serious failures, not totally unexpected on a wooden boat nearly a quarter of a century old. The swift 40 ft Finisterre class yawl had been built to the high specifications of her original American owner by a Portuguese yard in 1953. By the time Erick bought her in Le Havre, *Calao* had been badly neglected, but her elegant lines appealed to him so much,

The crew of *Calao* having fun in Vava'u, Tonga. Muriel is swiftly lifted out of the water by *Calao*'s 1000 sq ft spinnaker.

that he fell in love with her and within two years declared her ready to take on the oceans of the world. He folded up his successful insurance agency and with wife Muriel, daughter Sidonie, who was five at the time and son Fabien, only two, they set off on a long voyage which both Erick and Muriel wanted to do and enjoy while they were still young.

During the first winter of cruising in the Caribbean we often met by chance, until one evening when I described my plans of visiting the United States during the hurricane season in the Caribbean.

'That sounds very tempting,' replied Erick, who until then had been thinking of spending the season somewhere completely different. Obviously a detour of several thousand miles meant nothing to him, something that he later demonstrated on several occasions. He could change long established plans at the drop of a hat and, with his infectious enthusiasm, never had any trouble in getting Muriel to go along with the change. I soon found that Erick was game for any hairbrained idea, as long as it was crazy enough, such as night diving for lobster, salvaging useless stuff from sunken wrecks, crossing New York on folding bicycles, or spinnaker flying over an anchorage constantly visited by sharks. Anchoring *Calao* by the stern the spi-rider sat in the bosun's chair attached to the spinnaker, which let out on the halyard billows out like a parachute over the water.

'Having a fixed itinerary and then sticking to it, is about the most stupid thing one can do in this free life of ours,' he once said, while we were discussing which route to take after the United States and the Caribbean. I had already told him of my intention to sail down the coast of South America to Peru and thence to Easter Island. 'Oh, no, that's one place you won't find me,' he replied firmly. 'I have absolutely no desire to battle with the strength of the Humboldt current, when I can have an easy sail to the Marquesas.' We parted wakes in North Carolina, not sure when we would meet again, as we were planning to move at a faster rate than *Calao*. I was not too surprised however to discover that *Calao* had followed us to Peru, the temptation of seeing that part of the world being irresistible to such globe trotters as Erick and Muriel.

After spending the cyclone season in New Zealand, we decided to stay another year in the South Pacific and make a long detour to be in Tarawa for the Gilbert Islands' Independence Celebrations. By letter Erick and I decided *Aventura*'s track from New Zealand to the Gilberts could well intercept *Calao*'s track from Tahiti to Australia and we chose a suitable rendez-vous in Vava'u, Tonga. We surpassed even our own expectations by arriving at the rendez-vous only two hours apart.

Not having seen each other for over a year we easily filled the days swapping tales and gently cruising among the many islands of the Tongan archipelago. Work and mail however was waiting for me in Western Samoa, so I tried to persuade the Bouteleux to sail there as well, promising to take them out to dinner at Aggie Grey's famous hotel to celebrate Gwenda's birthday.

The weather was bad as we sailed out of Vava'u with headwinds and the promise of worse to come. On one of the tacks we got close enough together for me to shout across to Erick, that as they had recently sailed down from Samoa, they should carry on west and wait for us in Wallis, as they had originally planned. As darkness fell we lost sight of *Calao*. It took us five days of hard unpleasant sailing to cover the 300 odd miles to reach Samoa, so later the same day I couldn't believe it when *Calao* swept into Apia under full sail.

'Why on earth did you fight your way here, when you could have had a pleasant sail to Wallis?' I shouted across to Erick, incapable of hiding my surprise. It was his turn to look surprised.

'But, Jimmy, didn't you invite me to dinner? Surely you don't think we would miss an invitation to Aggie Grey's, do you?' At least it was worth the passage, as the same evening we sat down to an excellent dinner in the unique atmosphere of Aggie Grey's, the best known hotel in the South Pacific, run with unparalleled panache by this spritely lady eighty years young.

In Wallis, we separated again, this time agreeing to meet the following year in Australia. It was a meeting *Calao* almost never made. While sailing from Wallis to Futuna, two French territories in the Central Pacific, *Calao* encountered bad weather with mountainous seas. She fell into a deep trough and split a seam, the boat barely making the lee of Futuna with water gushing in through the open seam.

While *Aventura* spent the following cyclone season in Papua New Guinea, *Calao* chose the dry climate of Queensland so that Erick could restore his wooden decks. We arranged to meet in Cairns and sail to join an armada of traditional canoes sailing along the coast of Papua to Port Moresby as part of the Pacific Festival of Arts.

It was late on the day of our rendez-vous when I saw the familiar shape of *Calao* down the river at Cairns. The boat seemed to be making very slow progress and then I saw that Erick was sitting in his Optimist dinghy and with his small outboard motor towing *Calao* behind him. I jumped in my dinghy to help.

'What has happened?' I asked.

'Oh, nothing much, we had to buck the current as the tide was running out. The oil pressure warning lamp came on, but as we were in the middle of the narrow channel with so much shipping, I didn't stop the engine. So it seized up.' Erick shrugged his shoulders. 'Still I kept the rendez-vous, didn't I?'

Closer inspection at anchor revealed that without oil, the engine had well and truly seized up. He also discovered that he could not get the spare parts for his Peugeot engine in Australia and that they would have to be ordered from France. Erick is not easily daunted.

'We'll opt out of following the Armada in and out of the reef along the Papuan coast, but I don't want to miss the Festival, so we will sail straight to Port Moresby. If Captain Cook could sail up the Barrier reef without an engine, so can I.' I refrained from pointing out that we were not all that far from where Cook's *Endeavour* ran aground, and *Calao* sailed uneventfully the 500 miles to Port Moresby, where the spare parts eventually arrived from Paris. At least Erick absolved himself for his grave error of disregarding the warning lamp, by repairing and reassembling the engine completely unaided. His unique talent of improvisation had always impressed me, hardly any job being too difficult for his well stocked workshop, set up in the oversized sail locker in *Calao*'s bows. In spite of the tremendous amount of maintenance work required by such an old wooden boat, *Calao* was always kept in spotless condition with gleaming topsides and brilliantly varnished spars.

Far from being a purist in the true sense of the word, Erick is a perfectionist when it comes to sailing his boat. Although equipped with selfsteering and an autopilot, on passage he rarely reads and likes to spend his time sitting in the cockpit physically enjoying the sailing and the water rushing past the hull. He sails the 40 ft *Calao* as though he was in a dinghy race. The sails are always perfectly trimmed for maximum efficiency and when the wind drops, up goes the 1000 sq ft spinnaker, *Calao* being one of the few cruising boats on which a spinnaker is constantly used. It is the one sail, for which the entire crew has to lend a hand, while young Sidonie and Fabien have sole responsibility for the mizzen staysail.

The childrens' education has taxed both parents to the limit, especially in the case of Fabien, who had no idea of school discipline and regarded the boat and the sea as his natural playground. While his son was younger, Erick had rigged a continuous wire around the wide side decks, along which Fabien would run incessantly like a dog on a lead, working off his excess energy. When he reached the age of five, morning play had to give way to school work, a daily task the purpose of which Fabien refused to comprehend. On many mornings I could hear Erick's exasperated voice booming out across the anchorage, 'Two and three make five. Five, do you understand? Five, like the fingers on your hand, you twit!'

Two terms in an Australian school, while Erick and Muriel prepared *Calao* for the long return to Europe, did wonders for the childrens' education. It also brought about an odd change, for they ceased to speak French to each other and would argue incessantly with a genuine Aussie twang.

As the children grew and Sidonie started approaching secondary school age, a return to France became a prospect which could no longer be ignored. *Calao*'s westward track became less erratic and after leaving Torres Straits behind, *Calao* headed for Indonesia, and yet another rendezvous with *Aventura*. We had already been sailing for over one month among the Indonesian islands and had arrived one week before the agreed date in Bali. On the appointed day, not expecting Bouteleux to yet again show up on time, we had already locked up the boat and were preparing to go ashore when *Calao* sailed slowly into Benoa. They dropped anchor next to us and when Erick saw that we were all packed up ready to go, called across,

'Give us ten minutes and we'll come too.'

'No hurry,' I replied, 'take your time, we can go tomorrow.'

'Why tomorrow? What's wrong with today?'

Indeed within ten minutes they were all ashore ready to join us in a three day trip to the interior of the island, as if they had just sailed across the bay and not a distance of over 1000 miles. There are many outstanding people among the cruising fraternity and Erick Bouteleux is only one of them, but whatever other qualities he may have, he certainly knows how to keep an appointment.

Calao leaving Singapore at the beginning of a long cruise in the Indian Ocean.

A Final Word

The stories interspersed among the foregoing chapters describe only a handful of people, whose personal experiences were considered to illustrate a particular point. In fact, the number of outstanding people, whom I have met during my travels was far greater and I am able to present only the quintessence of their knowledge in these pages. As Eric Hiscock told me himself, however much one knows about the sea and sailing, one can still learn a lot from others; so I have been the first person to benefit from the information and suggestions that came my way. While such tips and advice have been of great use to me in a practical way, the attitudes of certain sailors have greatly influenced my own way of thinking and looking at things. My first mentor was the Italian singlehander Mario Franchetti, whose boat *Coconasse* was a perfect example of effortless sailing combined with maximum comfort and security. Albert Steele and Mike Bales have taught me the virtue of patience, while Susan and Eric Hiscock that of modesty. From Chester Lemon I learned that on a boat, nothing should be impossible and everything can be fixed, while Erick and Muriel Bouteleux have shown me more than once the true meaning of friendship.

In an increasingly impersonal world, it is reassuring to see the great generosity shown by many members of the cruising fraternity to each other. Ashore too there are still many people in various parts of the world, who shower their generosity upon the crews of visiting boats, usually without expecting anything in return. They are proud to be hosts to a fellow human being who has had the courage to set off across the oceans in a small boat to visit their distant shores. However, with more and more people taking to the sea, a long voyage by small boat is no longer regarded such an unusual feat as to merit special recognition and the reception given to the voyager is often becoming less enthusiastic.

This is an aspect which I have discussed at length with some of the older crews, who can still remember, with justified nostalgia, the days when they hardly ever had to share an anchorage with another boat and were received everywhere with utmost warmth and friendliness. These sailors also pointed to a gradual change that has occurred over recent years in small boat voyagers, from seafarers to sightseers. More and more people take to the sea as a means of seeing the world and not just for the love of sailing. The one thing they have in common, sailors and tourists alike, is still the mode of transport and because of that, certain rules of the sea have to be obeyed by all. A desire to see the world is certainly a valid reason for putting to sea in a small boat, as long as the basic tenets of seamanship and navigation are not ignored.

What I feel is wrong is to bring to the sea some of the attitudes of modern mass tourism. Although the majority of voyagers behave in a responsible and considerate fashion, there are unfortunately a few whose attitudes towards both officials and locals in foreign countries spoil the scene for all those who follow behind. It is mostly these selfish attitudes which have brought about the change deplored by those who were fortunate enough to cruise the world two or three decades ago. The reception given by local people is often less friendly than in the past, while some yacht clubs will no longer extend the customary hospitality to visiting crews, usually because someone had left with unpaid bills or had abused club facilities.

An even more disturbing trait that is noticeable among a few sailing people, apart from a lack of honesty and consideration, is that of racial prejudice. I was stunned to hear a skipper call the immigration officer in Tahiti 'boy', or a young sailor refer to the customs officers in Sri Lanka as 'stupid niggers'. During a traditional welcoming ceremony in Fiji, the crew of one yacht refused to shake hands with the island chief, because he was black, after which the attitude of the villagers towards all visitors became markedly cool. In a small port in Malaysia it took only one skipper to insult an immigration official and two years later visiting crews could still not get more than a two week extension to their visas, while elsewhere they could get up to three months. It does indeed take only a few such rotten apples to spoil the barrel for all of us who follow in their wake. Such examples have only been included to show that having a sound boat and being a good sailor does not preclude the need to also have a large amount of common-sense and consideration for others.

Commonsense is something that should dictate not only one's relation-ship with people on other boats and ashore, but also the kind of boat one chooses and the way everything is prepared for the intended voyage. The choice of boat is one area where a wrong decision can put the entire voyage in jeopardy later on. Unfortunately it is one decision which by necessity most people have to make before acquiring the cruising experience, which may well dictate entirely new priorities. It is the reason who so many skippers stressed the overriding importance of trying to get one's priorities right from the beginning. I should point out perhaps that most of the people I interviewed are the success stories, which were often matched by at least an equal number of failures and abandoned voyages. The wrong type of boat was often specified as the prime cause of such failures. It is a pitfall however that can be avoided by considering carefully from the beginning two important factors, the age and size of the crew and the area to be cruised.

Too small a boat with a crew that includes small children, can become unacceptably crammed as the voyage progresses and the children are growing. Similarly too large a boat for those who may lose part of the crew en route, or may become physically less able to handle it as they get older, can be equally frustrating.

The area where one is likely to spend most of the time should also have a bearing on the choice of boat. If one plans to follow the trade wind route around the world, the windward capabilities of the boat are not crucial, but if one intends to do a lot of zigzagging across the weather systems, a boat that can go well to windward is essential. A powerful and reliable engine can be just as important if one intends to explore out of the way places and reef areas. A moderate draft can also prove to be an advantage in such areas, as could the choice of a multihull.

After writing about the loss of cruising boats, I have been often asked about the safety of small boat voyaging. It is of course impossible to assess the overall safety of small boat voyaging, but the onus of safe cruising lies very much in the hands of each individual. Exactly as in motoring, where one can minimise the chances of an accident by driving carefully, taking avoiding action in good time, obeying the rules of the road and having a safe car, so on a boat one can apply the same principles, with the added advantage that most of the time one's life is not put at risk by the bad driving habits of others. After thousands of miles and many years of sailing, I have reached the conclusion that sailing is as safe as we ourselves make it, because ultimately the safety of our lives is most of the time in our own hands. In the words of the Welsh poet, W H Davies,

> 'I am the Master of my fate.
> I am the Captain of my soul.'

Being the master of one's own fate is for me one of the main attractions of long distance cruising.

Appendix A: The Surveys

THE SUVA SURVEY

No.	Name of Boat	Home Port	Country	Design	Rig	Mat	LOD	Crew	Place most liked
1	Eryx II	Gibraltar	Gibraltar	Camper & Nich.	Sc	S	78	4	Marquesas
2	Constellation	San Diego	USA	Alden	Sc	W	76	8	Fiji
3	Mandalay	Seattle	USA	R. Perry CT 54	K/s	G	54	3	Philippines
4	Spellbound II	Dartmouth	UK	A. Buchanen	K/s	W	52	3	Galapagos
5	Merry Maiden	Boston	USA	P. Rhodes	K	W	52	4	Easter Island
6	La Bohême	San Francisco	USA	Force 50	K/s	G	51	4	Lesser Antilles
7	Integrity	Hawaii	USA	E. McInnes	K	W	50	5	Tahiti
8	Mac's Opal	Coos Bay	USA	Samson Seabreeze	K/s	F	49'9	2	Ahe
9	Mortail	San Francisco	USA	Guy Beach/tri	K	P	47	3	Fiji
10	Enchantress	Hawaii	USA	Wellington 47	K/s	G	47	5	Fiji
11	Galatea IV	Vancouver	Canada	C. Kennedy	C	G	47	3	Vava'u
12	Sea Swan	New York	USA	A. Corener	Sc	W	46'6	3	Tahiti
13	Antigone	San Francisco	USA	Piver 46/tri	K	P	46	4	Vava'u
14	Con Tina	Los Angeles	USA	Cal 2-46	K	G	46	2	Bora Bora
15	Jolly II Roger	Portland	USA	Cal 2-46	K	G	46	2	W. Samoa
16	Whistler	Lyons	USA	Cal 2-46	K	G	46	2	Suvorov
17	Honeymead	Brisbane	Australia	Roberts Offshore	K/s	G	44	2	Alaska
18	Norseman	Long Beach	USA	Block Island	C	W	42	2	Hawaii
19	Aminadab	Santa Barbara	USA	Westsail	C	G	42	2	Tahiti
20	Rhodora	Key West	USA	R. Perry	C	G	42	2	Papua New Guinea
21	Caravela of Exe	Exeter	UK	Alden 42	Y	G	42	2	Fiji
22	Sarrie	Auckland	NZ	CT 41	K	G	41	4	Spain
23	Kaunis Uni	Juno	USA	Piver AA/tri	Sl	P	41	3	Alaska

No.	Name	Port	Country	Designer	LOA			Rig	Cruising from/to
24	Hägar	Sydney	Australia	J. Adams	40	2	S	C	Suvorov
25	Fair Lady	San Francisco	USA	L. Giles	40	3	W	C	Fiji
26	Tikitere	Auckland	NZ	B. Donovan	40	2	F	K/s	Fiji
27	Whale's Tale II	Hawaii	USA	Islander 40	40	4	G	K	Fiji
28	Gitana del Mar	San Diego	USA	Garden Gulf	40	3	G	Sl	Rarotonga
29	Camdella	Napier	NZ	Herreshoff	38	3	W	Sl	Makongai/Fiji
30	Riptide	Kimbe	PNG	S & S 38	38	3	A	Sl	Carolines
31	Akahi	Hawaii	USA	Cross 38/tri	38	2	W	K	Costa Rica
32	Taurewa	Nelson	NZ	R. Perry	37	2	G	C	Fiji
33	Hero	Portsmouth	USA	Mariner 36	36	2	G	C	Hawaii
34	Spindrift	Melbourne	Australia	Almsemgeeste	36	4	S	C	Fiji
35	Active Light	Pt. Townsend	USA	Atkin Tallyho	36	2	G	C	Vava'u
36	Coryphena	San Diego	USA	Hanna Carol	36	2	W	K	Suvorov
37	Sea Foam	Newport Beach	USA	Seawitch	36	3	W	K/s	Suvorov
38	Sea Rover	Manele/Hawaii	USA	Seawitch	36	2	W	K/s	Papeete
39	Super Roo II	Newport Beach	USA	Eriksson 36	36	4	G	C	Lord Howe
40	Swan	Portland	USA	Cascade 36	36	2	G	Sl	Vava'u
41	Warna Carina	Perth	Australia	Randall	36	5	F	K	Indonesia
42	Karak	Morlaix	France	Knocker	35'6	2	S	K	Lesser Antilles
43	Windrose	Vancouver	Canada	Nicholson 35	35'3	2	G	Sl	San Blas
44	Banjeeri	Newcastle	Australia	Randall	35	2	S	Sl	New Zealand
45	Lorbas	Köln	Germany	Kirk	35	2	G	Sl	Tuamotus
46	Olive Marie	Oxnard	USA	Garden 35	35	2	G	K/s	New Hebrides
47	Ranger	Victoria	Canada	Garden 35	35	2	W	K/s	French Polynesia
48	UFO II	Arnhem	Netherlands	Telstar/tri	35	2	G	Sl	Madeira
49	No name	Hawaii	USA	Robb 35	35	3	G	Sl	Suyorov
50	Hibiscus	Witianga	NZ	Woolacott	34	2	W	K/s	North Island/NZ

No.	Name of Boat	Home Port	Country	Design	Rig	Mat	LOD	Crew	Place most liked
51	Jocelyn	Newport Beach	USA	Lapworth	Sl	G	33'3	2	Tahiti
52	Kemana	Vancouver	Canada	Brewer 32	Sl	G	32	2	Ahe
53	Noa Noa	Miami	USA	P. Rhodes	K	W	32	2	Suvorov
54	Horizon	Stowe	USA	Golden Hind	Sl	P	31'6	3	Marquesas
55	Lou IV	Elmshorn	Germany	Jensen	K	G	31	2	Moorea
56	Runestaff	Whangerei	NZ	Herreshoff	C	G	29'7	2	Aitutaki
57	Ben Gunn	Wellington	NZ	Herreshoff	Sl	G	29	2	Virginia
58	Pink Mola Mola	Tokyo	Japan	Nakayoshi	Sl	G	28'9	1	Bora Bora
59	Alonda	Brisbane	Australia	Hartley Tasman	Sl	F	27'3	2	Fiji
60	Sara III	Stockholm	Sweden	Grinde	Sl	G	27	2	Galapagos
61	Lookfar	Seattle	USA	Westerly Centaur	Sl	G	26	2	Lau/Fiji
62	Jonathan	San Francisco	USA	Columbia	Sl	G	24	2	Palmyra

Rig: K = ketch
K/s = staysail ketch
Sc = schooner
Sl = sloop
C = cutter
Y = yawl

Material: S = steel
G = fibreglass or foam sandwich
W = wood
P = plywood
F = ferrocement
A = light alloy

2. THE CRUISING SURVEY

No.	Name of boat	Home Port	Country	Design	Rig	LOD	Crew	Length of cruise Yrs	Miles	Skipper
1	Orplid	Bremen	Germany	One off	K	56	2	3	22000	Rolf Stukenberg
2	Starshine	San Francisco	USA	Own	K	56	2+1	1½	8000	Doug Balcombe
3	Wanderlust	Sacramento	USA	Veleo 55	C	55	6	1½	10000	Steve Carter
4	Merry Maiden	Boston	USA	P. Rhodes	K	52	4	10	50000	Seaton Grass
5	Wanderer IV	Southampton	UK	Van der Meer	K	50	2	11	70000	Eric Hiscock
6	Mac's Opal	Coos Bay	USA	Seabreeze	K	50	2	3	30000	Royal McInness
7	Diogenes	Portland	USA	O. Stephens	K	50	3	5	48000	Gustaf Wollmar
8	Duen	St. Thomas/VI	USA	Norwegian FV	K	48	2+2	8	50000	Albert Fletcher
9	Hawk	Miami	USA	Adams	Sc	48	2	1½	18000	Dud Dewey
10	Alkinoos	La Rochelle	France	Nicholson 48	K	48	2	3	24000	Jean-Fr. Delvaux
11	Galatea IV	Vancouver	Canada	C. Kennedy	C	47	3	1½	10000	Bob Miller
12	Roscop	Antwerp	Belgium	Martens	K	46	2	2½	15000	Rein Mortier
13	Korong II	Brisbane	Australia	Own	K	43	2+2	2	10000	John Holmes
14	Canard Laqué	Basle	Switzerland	Luders Clipper	K	42	2	8	55000	Pierre Graf
15	Aslan	San Diego	USA	Kettenburg	Sl	41	2	2	10000	Scott Wilmoth
16	Shangri-La	Hamburg	Germany	Hartz/cat	K	40	3	2	23000	Burghard Pieske
17	Hägar	Sydney	Australia	J. Adams	C	40	2	4	20000	Gunter Gross
18	Calao	Toulon	France	Finisterre	Y	40	2+2	3	22000	Erick Bouteleux
19	Wrangler	Durban	South Africa	Own	K	40	2	2	22000	Robert Millar
20	Tarrawarra	Melbourne	Australia	A. Payne	Sl	38	3	2	12000	Kim Prowd
21	Felix	Paimpol	France	Ophelie	K	38	2+1	3	25000	Alain Bloch

No.	Name of boat	Home Port	Country	Design	Rig	LOD	Crew	Length of cruise Yrs	Length of cruise Miles	Skipper
22	Incognito	Santa Barbara	USA	One off	Sl	38	2	5	22000	Steve Abney
23	Rising Sun	Los Angeles	USA	Lapworth	Sl	37	2	2	10000	Dan Bache-Wiig
24	Fortuna	Auckland	NZ	One off	C	37	2+2	7	50000	Mike Morrish
25	Peregrine	San Diego	USA	Berthan Gauntlet	C	37	1	3½	12000	Albert Steele
26	Gambol	Tauranga	NZ	One off	Sl	37	2	6	45000	Stuart Clay
27	Hero	Portsmouth	USA	R. Perry	C	36	2	2	10000	Richard Holcombe
28	Because	Victoria	Canada	One off	C	36	1	1½	10000	Dick Thulliers
29	Tern	Knysna	South Africa	One off	Sl	36	1	2	23000	John Travers
30	Sea Foam	Newport Beach	USA	Seawitch	K	36	3	6½	35000	Herb Payson
31	Karak	Morlaix	France	Knocker	K	35	2	3½	21000	Georges Calmé
32	Windrose	Vancouver	Canada	Nicholson 35	Sl	35	2	2	20000	Mik Madsen
33	Ranger	Victoria	Canada	Garden	K	35	2	3	14000	Gene Williams
34	Telemark	Southampton	UK	Buchanan Yeoman	Sl	35	2	12	50000	Alan Allmark
35	Jocelyn	Newport Beach	USA	Cal 34	Sl	33	2	2	10000	Jay Becker
36	Iemanja	San Francisco	USA	Luders	K	33	2	1½	15000	Grant Nielson
37	Potpourri	Hueneme	USA	Islander	C	32	2	1	10000	Al Huso
38	L'Orion	San Francisco	USA	Westsail	C	32	2+1	1½	8000	Don Lewis
39	Talofa Lee	San Francisco	USA	Westsail	C	32	2	1	10000	Dave Weikart
40	Kemana	Vancouver	Canada	Brewer	Sl	32	2	3	14000	Nick Zeldenrust
41	Spaciety	San Diego	USA	Kantola/tri	Sl	32	2	6	30000	Larry Pooter

42	Horizon	Stowe	USA	Golden Hind	Sl	31	2+1	$1\frac{1}{2}$	15000	Bruce MacDonald
43	Lou IV	Elmshorn	Germany	Jensen	K	31	2	3	30000	Herbert Gieseking
44	Tehani III	Antwerp	Belgium	West Hinder	Sl	31	1	2	23000	Jan Swerts
45	Macushlah	Honolulu	USA	Kittiwake	K	30	2	9	12000	Dave Malseed
46	Fawn of Chichester	Cowes	UK	Cavalier	Sl	30	2	2	20000	Roger Morgan
47	Runestaff	Whangerei	NZ	Herreshoff	C	29	2	4	16000	Ian Hancock
48	Tara II	Vancouver	Canada	Vancouver	Sl	27	2	2	8000	George Harley
49	Silverheels	San Diego	USA	Yankee	Sl	26	2	$1\frac{1}{2}$	8000	David Mancini
50	Jellicle	South Shields	UK	Folkboat	C	25	2	20	85000	Mike Bales

Rig:
K = ketch
C = cutter
Sc = schooner
Sl = sloop
Y = yawl

3. THE SEAWIVES SURVEY

No.	Name	Country	Boat	LOD	Yrs Present Cruise	Children on board Names (age)
1	Ruth Abney	NZ	Incognito	38	5	
2	Beryl Allmark	UK	Telemark	35	12	
3	Denny Bache-Wiig	USA	Rising Sun	37	2	
4	Linda Balcombe	USA	Starshine	56	$1\frac{1}{2}$	Heather (11)
5	Kathy Becker	USA	Jocelyn	33	2	
6	Betty Bloch	France	Felix	38	3	Yann (5)
7	Muriel Bouteleux	France	Calao	40	3	Sidonie (8), Fabien (5)
8	Hélène Calmé	France	Karak	35	$3\frac{1}{2}$	
9	Pamela Church	Zimbabwe	Gambol	37	3	
10	Jeannette Delvaux	France	Alkinoos	48	3	
11	Barbara Dewey	USA	Hawk	48	$1\frac{1}{2}$	
12	Dottie Fletcher	USA	Duen	48	8	Toby (13), James (11)
13	Illa Gieseking	Germany	Lou IV	31	3	
14	Ute Graf	Switzerland	Canard Laqué	42	8	
15	Derry Hancock	UK	Runestaff	29	4	Tristan (6 weeks)
16	Cynthia Hathaway	USA	Spaciety	32	2	
17	Suzanne Hartley	Canada	Tara II	27	2	
18	Susan Hiscock	UK	Wanderer IV	50	11	
19	Vicki Holmes	Australia	Korong II	43	2	Kirsty (5), Denby (3)
20	Karen Huso	USA	Potpourri	32	1	
21	Nancy Lewis	USA	L'Orion	32	$1\frac{1}{2}$	
22	Kay Malseed	USA	Macushlah	30	9	Daren (8)

23	Pat Mancini	USA	Silverheels	26	$1\frac{1}{2}$	
24	Lorraine Millar	South Africa	Wrangler	40	2	
25	Marg Miller	Canada	Galatea IV	47	1	
26	Anne Morrish	NZ	Fortuna	37	7	
27	Marie-Louise Mortier	Belgium	Roscop	46	$2\frac{1}{2}$	Paul (13), Tina (11)
28	Liz MacDonald	USA	Horizon	31	$1\frac{1}{2}$	
29	D'Ann McLain	USA	Windrose	35	2	Jeff (10)
30	Opal McInness	USA	Mac's Opal	50	3	
31	Donna Nielson	USA	Iemanja	32	1	
32	Nancy Payson	USA	Sea Foam	36	$6\frac{1}{2}$	
33	Carol Ritz	USA	Hero	36	2	
34	Helga Seebeck	Germany	Shangri-La	40	2	
35	Alice Simpson	UK	Fawn of Chichester	30	2	
36	Stefani Stukenberg	Germany	Orplid	56	3	
37	Blitz Weikart	USA	Talofa Lee	32	1	
38	Marie Williams	Canada	Ranger	35	3	
39	Beverly Wilmoth	USA	Aslan	41	2	
40	Britz Zeldenrust	Canada	Kemana	32	3	

4. THE CIRCUMNAVIGATORS SURVEY

No.	Boat	Crew	Country	Design	LOA	Material	Rig	Years	Mileage	Favourite Place
1	Alkinoos	Jeannette & Jean-François Delvaux	France	Camper & Nicholson	48	GRP	K	$4\frac{1}{2}$	45,000	Lesser Antilles
2	Barsoi	Heinz Lutz	Germany	S & S	30	GRP	Sl	4	36,000	French Polynesia
3	Ben Gunn	Tony Ray Kevin Oliver	NZ	Herreshoff	28	GRP	Sl	4	40,000	Virginia, USA
4	Gambol	Stuart Clay (Pam Church)	NZ	T. Coyte	37	W	Sl	6	40,000	Virgin Islands
5	Horizon	Liz & Bruce MacDonald & son Jeff	USA	Golden Hind	31	GRP on ply	Sl	3	33,500	Indonesia
6	Kyeri	Herb & Mary-Louise Stewart	USA	Hinckley-Owens	40	W	C	3	35,000	New Zealand
7	Lorbas	Achim & Irma Geysel	Germany	Amel	36	GRP	Sl	3	29,000	Tuamotus
8	Lou IV	Herbert & Ilse Gieseking	Germany	Compass Jensen	31	GRP	K	$4\frac{1}{2}$	46,000	Solomon Islands
9	Pomona	Ian & Sylvia French & son John	UK	Colin Cowen	27	W	Sl	3	31,000	Cocos Keeling
10	Sara III	Christer & Britt Fredriksson	Sweden	P. Bruun	26	GRP	Sl	5	50,000	Melanesia
11	Tivia	Doncho & Julie Papazov & daughter Yana	Bulgaria	Polish one off	45	W	K	2	40,500	French Polynesia
12	Windrose	Mik Madsen (D'Ann McLain)	Canada	Nicholson	35	GRP	Sl	$3\frac{1}{4}$	47,000	San Blas

Appendix B: Cooking Fuel

Although the internal features of cruising boats were not considered in the surveys, which form the basis of this book, I tried at least to find an answer to the controversial question of cooking fuel. In the Suva survey I found that 53 per cent of the sixty-two boats surveyed used bottled gas and the high average rating of 9·35 indicated that the users were happy with this fuel, although most of them specified that adequate safety measures were essential. The 39 per cent users of paraffin (kerosene) seemed less satisfied, giving it a rating of 7·95. Four of the boats in the Suva survey used electricity (110 V) in the galley and were equipped with powerful generators for this reason. Electricity as a cooking fuel received an average rating of 9, while the only user of methylated spirit rated it at 6.

An increasing number of cruising boats are using gas for cooking and from what I was told, no great problems were encountered in having containers filled in any of the main islands of the Pacific or the Caribbean, where this fuel is used extensively by the local population. More problems seem to be encountered in the Mediterranean by boats equipped with non-European type containers. Unfortunately gas containers have not been standardised internationally, and both their capacity and valve fittings often vary from country to country. This can present some problems when the container has to be re-filled; some filling stations have the necessary adaptors for all major systems, while some cautious skippers carry these adaptors on board.

The containers can be used for either propane or butane gas, propane being the fuel more generally available in tropical countries, and this can cause damage to burners on cookers which have been designed for use with butane gas. These burners tend to burn out and have to be renewed more frequently. Also when changing from propane to butane, which is used more in temperate climates, it is wise to change the regulator or have its rating checked. The average consumption of gas is difficult to assess, but on most cruising boats an allowance of 10 lbs of gas per month seems more than adequate.

Index